How To Shine

**Insights into unlocking your
potential from proven winners**

Simon Hartley

CAPSTONE

This edition first published 2012
© 2012 Simon Hartley

Registered office
Capstone Publishing Ltd. (A Wiley Company), John Wiley and Sons Ltd, The
Atrium, Southern Gate, Chichester, West Sussex, PO19 8SQ, United Kingdom

For details of our global editorial offices, for customer services and for information
about how to apply for permission to reuse the copyright material in this book
please see our website at www.wiley.com.

Wiley publishes in a variety of print and electronic formats and by print-on-
demand. Some material included with standard print versions of this book may not
be included in e-books or in print-on-demand. If this book refers to media such as a
CD or DVD that is not included in the version you purchased, you may download
this material at http://booksupport.wiley.com. For more information about Wiley
products, visit www.wiley.com.

Designations used by companies to distinguish their products are often claimed as
trademarks. All brand names and product names used in this book are trade names,
service marks, trademarks or registered trademarks of their respective owners. The
publisher is not associated with any product or vendor mentioned in this book. This
publication is designed to provide accurate and authoritative information in regard
to the subject matter covered. It is sold on the understanding that the publisher is
not engaged in rendering professional services. If professional advice or other expert
assistance is required, the services of a competent professional should be sought.

Library of Congress Cataloging-in-Publication Data

Hartley, Simon.
  How to shine : insights into unlocking your potential from proven winners /
Simon Hartley.
      p. cm.
  Includes bibliographical references and index.
  ISBN 978-0-857-08358-6 (pbk.) – ISBN 978-0-857-08359-3 (ebk) –
ISBN 978-0-857-08361-6 (ebk) – ISBN 978-0-857-08360-9 (ebk)
  1. Success.   2. Success in business.   3. Self-confidence.
  4. Self-management (Psychology)   I. Title.
  BF637.S8H3328 2012
  650.1–dc23
                                                                    2012024369

A catalogue record for this book is available from the British Library.

ISBN 978-0-857-08358-6 (paperback) ISBN 978-0-857-08360-9 (ebk)
ISBN 978-0-857-08361-6 (ebk)   ISBN 978-0-857-08359-3 (ebk)

Cover design – Binary & The Brain

Set in 11/14 pt ACaslon Pro-Regular by Toppan Best-set Premedia Limited,
Hong Kong
Printed in Great Britain by TJ International Ltd, Padstow, Cornwall, UK

Contents

Foreword   vii
Preface   xi
Acknowledgements   xiii

Introduction   1
1   Have A Dream   15
2   Focus On The Next Step   35
3   Keep It Simple   51
4   Don't Compromise   63
5   Push The Envelope   83
6   Be Mentally Tough   103
7   Take Responsibility, Take Control   123
8   Be Yourself   135
9   Be The Best You Can Be   151

Bibliography   171
About Simon Hartley   179
Index   181

Foreword

I have spent my business career seeking to build and develop great teams which can focus and organize themselves to achieve outstanding results. I have been a member of great teams and have seen in those teams extraordinary performers who appear to shine and by doing so illuminate the performance and motivation of the whole team. Those individuals are the gold dust, the glitter which catalyzes a very good team to produce a unit able to produce consistently exceptional results. When I see someone who shines I can recognize the talent and appreciate that I have to nurture the individual and their talent as they will raise the performance of my whole business. In my own amateur and unsystematic way, I have sought to understand what it is that makes these people shine, why and how they can perform consistently to the highest level and provide a benchmark for others to aspire to.

In my bid to understand how to develop and support world class performers, I want to know what sets the truly exceptional apart from the very good because, in today's massively competitive world, to be only very good is to be invisible. An individual, team or organization only achieves true strength from being the best, demonstrating quality, defining and applying excellence in all areas. Some individuals appear to be able to do just that. But if we can identify the truly outstanding performers – the people who really do shine – a series of questions then raise themselves. What is it that actually sets the exceptional performers apart? How do we recognize real talent, identify those who have the ability and desire to be the best? Those who have the focus and determination to create excellence?

If we can identify these outstanding individuals – or those destined to become exceptional – how can we support their development and help them to continue to develop their outstanding performance?

The first question usually asked in this regard is whether it is nature or nurture which encourages individuals to become extraordinary achievers? Are extraordinary people born gifted or can you learn what it takes to achieve extraordinary results? Or is it luck? The right place at the right time? Or is it a mixture of all of these things? Are extreme high achievers driven to escape their surroundings or are they striving to reach a goal?

This book sets out to explore and provide answers to some of those questions as they apply to world class performers from a range of backgrounds, professions and activities – commercial, professional and sporting. In discussing and exploring the views and experiences of world class performers the author exposes the reader to the reasoning and philosophy of those who shine, who achieve world records and extraordinary success. The reader is invited to share their world, looking from the inside out and understanding, from their perspective, what differentiates extreme high achievers. What exactly are they chasing and what is it which motivates them to succeed, to reach the goal or to fight through difficulties and challenges. What role does personal energy and passion play? Does passion create energy, or the other way around, and is this enough to focus performance and achieve the result?

By investigating the reasons why those who shine believe they have been able to achieve world class performance and then by analysing their behaviour and beliefs the author is able to contrast the different viewpoint of the performer and the observer. By seeking trends, consistencies and shared beliefs and values we are given the opportunity to resolve the forces acting on these individuals and identify reasons why they have been able to achieve astonishing results.

If you want to understand how ordinary people can appreciate and respect the anticipated boundary of their own performance and then consistently surpass that boundary to achieve extraordinary results time after time then this book is for you.

**Kevin Gaskell, former Managing Director
of Porsche and BMW**

Preface

For many years I have had the great pleasure of working with world-class athletes and sports teams. Watching them live and work has raised questions in my mind. What is it that makes some people exceptional? What differentiates them from the ones who almost made it? These questions have intrigued me for years. At the turn of the year, I decided to interview a group of world-class people from a diverse range of fields. My rationale was pretty simple. If there are traits that are common to world-class chefs, mountaineers, baristas, athletes, polar explorers, special-forces personnel and scientists, those traits are likely to cross into any domain; in business and in life.

As a sport psychologist and performance coach, I have read many books that also set out to understand what differentiates the very best. However, a lot of these books didn't really get under the skin and help me understand the insights, experiences and perspectives of world-class people. I want to know how these people think, how they make their decisions, how they approach situations and respond to the challenges that they encounter.

Therefore, the approach taken in this book is quite different from the majority of sport psychology, personal development or business performance publications. It is based on the thoughts, opinions and experiences of a diverse range of people who have reached the very pinnacle of their fields. It focuses heavily on lived experiences, rather than being driven by theory. An insight into lived experience is often more tangible and easier to apply. The experiences of these particular people are also hugely inspirational.

As I have written this book, I have made a conscious effort to present the accounts of these incredible people in quite a raw state and, where possible, to let you read their words. One of those interviewed is a twice Michelin-starred chef. He talks about the need to let the ingredients speak for themselves and not to interfere too much. I have tried to follow that philosophy myself.

I truly hope that you find the material as valuable and inspiring as I have. The process and journey that I have taken, whilst writing this book, has been amazing. I have worked alongside many world-class athletes over the last 15 years and learned a huge amount from them. However, I could never have imagined just how much I would learn from those I interviewed. Their insights have taught me more than I could dare to have dreamed. I have learned an incredible amount and I hope that you do too.

Acknowledgements

I would like to thank all those who have contributed to this book. In particular, I offer my sincere appreciation to the world-class people who agreed to be interviewed.

Kenny Atkinson
Linda Conlon
Chris Cook
Bruce Duncan
Alan Hinkes
James Hoffmann
Andy McMenemy
Chris Robertson
Gary Rossi
Ben Saunders
Alison Waters
Keir Worth

I can honestly say that they are not just high achievers, but also fantastic people. It has been a privilege getting to know them. I am also very grateful to Kevin Gaskell for contributing the Foreword to this book and to Jonathan, Jenny and the team at Capstone for all their help

I also thank my gorgeous wife and fabulous girls, my parents, family, friends and all those who have supported me over the years. They continually pick me up, dust me down and help me back on my way!

I'd like to dedicate this book to my late mother-in-law, Anne, who is always in our thoughts.

Finally, thank you for reading this book. I wish you the very best in your journey and hope this book can be a valuable aid.

Introduction

Why did you pick up this book? Was it just curiosity, or is there a part of you that strives to truly excel in what you do? Do you have a burning desire to be the best you can possibly be?

Although this book is called *How To Shine*, it could easily have been titled *Be The Best You Can Be*. Many of us do aspire to be the best in our fields. Regardless of our profession, we like to feel that we can excel at what we do. Ambitious people are always looking for ways to improve themselves and get closer to their goals. This book will provide a valuable resource for anyone who wants to become a genuine leader in their field. Many organizations and individuals now realize that being average, in today's climate, equals vulnerable. Recently I have become aware that size is no guarantee of success, or even survival. Perhaps true strength comes from quality, not size. I believe that sentiment is true in sport, business and many other walks of life. Therefore, many people are now looking at ways to become exceptional and to truly shine! Striving to truly excel is a fantastic strategy for those who want to succeed in life.

So What Does Excellence Look Like?

One way to assess 'excellence' is to use an external benchmark, such as international recognition. Perhaps the easiest examples are seen in sports. Most sports have Olympic Champions or World Champions. They may also have world-ranking systems based on the accumulation of tournament points or prize money. In some cases, you would have to be a national champion even to qualify for a world competition.

International recognition is not just limited to sport. There are world championships in many disciplines outside of sport. Even disciplines such as making coffee have a world championship. There are also world records, which provide us with a way of knowing who has achieved the greatest feats in the world in each discipline. Some world records tell of incredible levels of human achievement. To achieve other world records, you may need to simply be the tallest man or woman on the planet. Ranking systems, like those used in golf, tennis and squash, are not just restricted to sports. Many areas of life, such as science, medicine and music, also have ranking systems that tell us who is best. Equally, we have acclaimed bodies that recognize the world's best for us. Bodies such as these give us Nobel Prize winners, Turner prize winners and Michelin star chefs.

However, there are many walks of life that do not necessarily have a clear-cut way of recognizing excellence. It's tough to do in business. The company with the highest turnover, or even profit, may not be the best. The organization with the highest number of members may not be the best. The product with the highest number of sales may not be the best either. Which recruitment consultancy is the best in the world? How would we tell? What criteria would we use? What would we measure? To my knowledge, there are no Michelin star equivalents in the recruitment sector. Measurement is relatively easy in sport, but in many walks of life it is not.

In many disciplines, it is the quality of their processes, which differentiate world-class operators from the rest. Simply put, there are some who do their job better than others. There are people and organizations throughout the world that are exceptionally good at what they do. These people often go unrecognized. In some cases, they might be world-class. You may walk past their door every day, or be queued behind them in a traffic jam and not even know it. Being exceptionally good in your field, does not necessarily mean that you are famous. Even many world-class people are not household names. Equally, there are many famous people who do not truly excel. I genuinely believe that aspiring to achieve our potential is a quest that is open to us all. It is not exclusive. It isn't restricted to a select number of privileged individuals or those who operate in specific domains. Simply doing your job better than others does provide a valid route to becoming excellent for many people. I'd also argue that it is an incredibly worthwhile mission.

In my quest to understand what characterizes those who truly are world-class, I have interviewed a diverse range of people, each of whom is at the very top of their field. In most cases, they have received external, international recognition. They are world champions, medal winning athletes, world-ranked sports players, chefs with multiple Michelin stars to their name, world record breakers, members of elite special-forces teams or leaders of world-class organizations. However, many of them are not particularly famous outside of their field. They are not widely recognized household names. You might walk down the street next to these people and not realize that you were rubbing shoulders with the world's best. However, they are all exceptional in their field:

Kenny Atkinson, twice Michelin-starred chef – by the age of 34, Kenny had been awarded two Michelin stars and he is currently working on a third. He has twice been a winner of the BBC television series the *Great British Menu* and was also named Chef of the Year 2009 at The Cateys, the catering industry's most fiercely competed awards.

Chris Cook, double Olympian and Commonwealth champion – Chris is a double Olympian swimmer who also has two Commonwealth gold medals, plus a European and World Championship bronze to his name. As he retired, Chris was the seventh fastest man in history in his event.

Keir Worth, England Squash's Head of Performance, and Chris Robertson, England Squash's National Head Coach – England has dominated world squash for the last 15 years winning five World Team Championships, winning 29 of the 30 European Championships and topping the Commonwealth Games medal table. In 2011, England had three top ten ranked players in both the men's and women's game.

James Hoffmann, World Barista Champion – James was crowned World Barista Champion in 2007 and then went on to coach the World Champions of 2008 and 2009. He also won the UK Barista Championships twice in consecutive years, making him the most successful competitive barista in the UK.

Bruce Duncan, Team GB captain and world-leading adventure racer – Bruce captained Team GB to three consecutive victories in the Wenger Patagonian Expedition Race. The Wenger, a 600 kilometer tri-discipline race through the Chilean Andes, is one of the world's toughest races.

Alison Waters, England International and world number 3 squash player – as an England International, Alison won the World Team Championships in 2006 and has twice won the European Team Championships. In January 2011, she ranked as the world number three squash player.

Alan Hinkes, OBE, world-leading mountaineer – Alan is one of only a dozen or so people in human history to have reached the summit of all 14 of the world's 8000 metre peaks.

Gary Rossi, retired US Navy SEAL Frogman and Bomb Squad Leader – Gary has also served as an Adjunct Professor for National University (NU) and San Diego State University (SDSU), teaching a variety of business performance, excellence and leadership courses.

Linda Conlon, Centre for Life Chief Executive – The Centre for Life is revolutionary within the world today. In 2005, scientists at the Centre for Life successfully cloned the first human embryo. The Centre for Life also hosts an internationally recognized Five Star research institution in Genetic Medicine.

Ben Saunders, record-breaking polar explorer – in 2004, Ben, aged 23, became the youngest person ever to reach the North Pole on foot. He is currently planning a world-record breaking unsupported return trek to the South Pole for 2012, which will be the longest unsupported polar journey in history.

Andy McMenemy, record-breaking ultra-distance runner – on his fiftieth birthday, Andy successfully completed a world record breaking 66 ultra-marathons in 66 days, in the 66 cities of the UK.

So what is it that makes these people and these organizations exceptional? What is it that separates them from the rest? What have they got, which has allowed them to perform these incredible feats, and achieve their extraordinary success? One possible explanation is that they have talent. Have these people been blessed with some innate gifts? Were they born with greater potential than the rest of us? Were they simply destined to become great? Or, is it possible that they are just like you and me in many ways? Is it their decisions, choices, thought-process and perspective that has made them exceptional?

In recent years, these questions have received a lot of attention from scientists and authors. Several writers, such as Geoff Colvin (2008), Matthew Syed (2011), Daniel Coyle (2009) and Malcolm Gladwell (2008), have expanded on the research of psychologist Karl Anders Ericsson. He proposes that practice, rather than talent, underpins expert performance. Former professional footballer, Rasmus Ankersen (2011), found that the world's great athletes often come from cultures that develop world-class practices. Management researcher, Jim Collins, found that successful organizations and individuals are often not blessed with any more 'luck'. He found that planning and preparation were more reliable differentiators than 'chance'.

Are These People Naturally Talented?

Twice Michelin-starred chef Kenny Atkinson never dreamed of being a chef when he was growing up. He had his sights set on becoming a pilot in the Royal Air Force. However, Kenny struggled academically and he left school without the required qualifications. Needing a job, he started working in the markets, on a fruit and vegetable stall. Shortly afterwards, his uncle offered Kenny a job washing the dishes in the kitchen of his restaurant. During busy periods, the chefs would enlist Kenny's help preparing ingredients. Gradually, he started to do more and more and began to really enjoy the buzz of the kitchen.

Olympic swimmer Chris Cook on the other hand, did not particularly stand out as a potential world-class swimmer during his junior years. In his own words, he showed all the signs of somebody who would 'fizzle out of the sport'. His best result at the national championship was 28th. Even into his early 20s, Chris was not an outstanding prospect. He did not make the North East of England Regional Performance Squad at his first attempt, so had to try again a year later. When he finally made it into the squad, he still hadn't made a national final and yet he still had aspirations of becoming an Olympian.

> "I remember my first ever session at Newcastle. I got in the water, did one of the hardest sessions I can remember, threw up, went home and cried to my Mam. I said I wasn't going back."
> **Chris Cook, double Olympian and Commonwealth champion, on making his first elite squad**

James Hoffmann's journey to becoming a barista happened 'by mistake'. He desperately needed a job, after having done a number of random things and ended up in a large department store demonstrating espresso machines. It was there that he started to develop a passion for making espresso and eventually became a trainer. Along the way, James met other top baristas, which sparked his interest in becoming a competitive barista. This influence ultimately resulted in James being crowned World Champion in 2007.

Retired US Navy SEAL Gary Rossi set out on his naval career hoping to be an aviator. However, he was separated from the other graduates and missed his graduation. During his additional time at the Academy, Gary met an instructor who opened up an opportunity at the SEAL Training School. That was Gary's route into the Special Forces.

So it seems that many of these people fell into their chosen field, almost by accident. Although Gary Rossi may have had designs on becoming a member of the US Navy, he didn't set out with his sights set on becoming a SEAL. Kenny's introduction into cooking was not deliberate. Equally, James Hoffmann didn't set out from an early age to become a barista. In fact, their journeys show that passion grows. It may start as an interest. However, as we follow our interest, a 'like' can become a 'love' and ultimately a passion.

When I first met world record-breaking ultra-distance runner Andy McMenemy I imagined that he'd always been an endurance athlete. However, the reality is very different. After being made redundant, Andy decided to start doing some of the things he had always said he would, which included running ultra-marathons. Incredibly, Andy McMenemy went from not being able to run five miles at age 45, to completing a world record 66 ultra-marathons in 66 days on his 50th birthday!

These accounts certainly don't tell of people that had amazing innate talents either. They do not seem to have been imparted with any extraordinary gifts at birth. Olympic swimmer Chris Cook hadn't even qualified for a national final at the age of 18 when he went to university. Physiologically and mechanically, he does not have the textbook build that you would associate with a world-class swimmer; for a start, he's under six foot tall! Kenny and Chris also show that you don't need a privileged start. Both of them have come from pretty modest starting points.

Do You Need to Be In The Right Place At The Right Time?

Some world-class people may have benefited from having an environment that helped start them on the road to success. In his book, *Outliers*, Malcolm Gladwell (2008), suggests that perhaps practice is not the only differentiator between those who achieve extraordinary success, and the rest. Gladwell also argues that environment plays a role. One of those that Malcolm Gladwell interviewed was Microsoft founder, Bill Gates. Gladwell suggests that Bill Gates' success cannot solely be put down to 'genius'. It is a point that Gates elaborated on during the TED (Technology, Education and Design) Conference in February 2009:

> *"What the book says is that if you get opportunities, which are partly a matter of luck and partly a matter of skill, those compound. So, when I was young I got to use computers; that was very lucky. I got to work at a computer company because I was pretty good. These senior people looked at my code and told me, 'Nah, that's not as good as it can be'. And so I got better. And then I had another experience where a great developer looked at my code and told me how to do it better. So it's a cycle, where luck and skill come and mess with each other and that's what leads to a great – from my point of view – a great outcome."*

World-class adventure racer Bruce Duncan grew up within a family of outdoor pursuits enthusiasts. His father was an Outdoor Activity instructor and his brother a Great Britain (GB) international orienteer and world relay champion. Bruce actually became an adventure racer after suffering an injury which ended his competitive life as an orienteer.

Mountaineer Alan Hinkes was born and raised in a town close to the North Yorkshire Moors and got the opportunity to trek in the hills whilst at school. Similarly, record-breaking polar explorer Ben Saunders grew up in the south west of England and spent a lot of time exploring places like Dartmoor. It seems that he also developed a love for the outdoors during his childhood:

"I used to read about explorers and adventurers. Lots of my role models were inspirational guys like Lance Armstrong and John Ridgway, the first to row the Atlantic. I loved walking and climbing. Although I moved quite a lot, I had six or seven different schools when I was a kid, I always loved the outdoors; it was my constant."

Ben Saunders, discussing what inspired him to become a polar explorer

So, it's clear to assume that the environment obviously did contribute to the journeys of Alan, Ben and Bruce. However, it can't be the only influence. There are thousands of people born and raised in the Lake District, Dartmoor and near the North Yorkshire Moors. Not all of them go on to become world-leading adventurers. Obviously, Alan, Ben and Bruce had opportunities that others may not have had access to, but those opportunities didn't automatically make them world-class. In fact, as Bill Gates' tale suggests, often world-class people seek those opportunities and then maximize them. Bill Gates was one of many people in his era that had access to a good education, computers and programming environments. Jim Collins (2011), highlights the fact that Gates made some decisions and some choices that ultimately led to his success. He decided to abandon his studies at Harvard, move to Albuquerque in New Mexico (where computer firm Altair were based) and work like a maniac to develop his first commercial software program. He actively sought the opportunities and then worked to develop them. So in these examples, 'talent' and 'opportunity' do not appear to give us the whole answer.

Is It A Combination Of Talent And Opportunity?

Maybe 'talent' plays a bigger role in certain fields? World number three squash player Alison Waters was part of a squash-playing family. She began playing squash at the age of five and was consistently one of the top English players from a young age. However, as Keir Worth, the Head of Performance at England Squash, points out, it is hard to know what constitutes natural talent, when athletes start playing at such a young age. Those that have good coaching and play at a high standard for many years are likely to rise to the top.

Chris Robertson, National Head Coach at England Squash, also offers his views on the significance of talent. He understands that there are some players that will find many elements of the game easy. For instance, perhaps they have a certain level of athleticism and move relatively easily, or better hand-eye coordination. However, the challenge is to be able to build on areas of strength, work on weaker areas and develop a complete game. Unfortunately, Chris sees many 'talented' juniors drop out of the sport when they face challenges. Those who find certain things easy, often don't know how to handle the tougher tests. In fact, having natural talent can actually be 'the kiss of death' for many players.

> *"It's very hard for them [highly talented players] to understand the holistic process, because they're winning and they're winning all the time. That's why you're looking for a player who looks past that. They use their talent but understand the rest . . . that means they have a strength, but also the attitude and understanding that it's not enough and they need to package up a more complete game."*
> **Chris Robertson, England Squash's**
> **National Head Coach**

Even the world's best are often not the most 'gifted'. For example, Chris described how world men's number one squash player, Nick Matthew, has worked incredibly hard to develop all the areas of his game. Although he may not have one area that he's particularly 'talented' in, Nick has been able to develop a very solid and complete game with very few weaknesses. So perhaps Nick Matthew's true talent is his ability to bring together all the elements of his game and become a complete player.

"I get uneasy when we talk about natural ability, because skills are learned."

Keir Worth, England Squash's
Head of Performance

When Michelin-starred chef Kenny Atkinson interviews junior chefs, he is not particularly interested in technical skills or even their palate. These things can be trained. Kenny is far more interested in their attitude and desire to succeed. In the past he has seen talented chefs who have not been team players, or had the desire to learn. Inevitably, those chefs don't excel. Therefore, Kenny looks for team players, who will listen, learn and are not afraid to work hard. In his more senior chefs, Kenny wants to see leadership and drive.

There appears to be a recurring theme. Talent and technical ability alone are not enough. In fact, in some cases they can actually be detrimental. Talented people tend to find that they pick things up more easily, develop more quickly and get results earlier than others. However, that does not always lead to success. By contrast, those who are less talented may develop other qualities by necessity. In order to keep pace with their talented counterparts, they may become more disciplined, resilient or determined. They learn to develop the skills they need, rather than relying on their innate talent alone.

"My greatest achievements came from working on the 80% of things that I wasn't very good at. If I was talented in those

things, I wouldn't have needed to work particularly hard on them."

Chris Cook, double Olympian and Commonwealth champion, discussing the role that talent played in his success

The very fact that the nature verses nurture debate has raged for centuries indicates that there is no clear-cut answer, and that quite possibly, the idea of either nature or nurture is folly. Arguably we all have talents. Perhaps we should look at what talents people have and how they can best employ them. Do we make the most of the talent we have? Do we build on them or pursue something that is unrelated to our talents? What these accounts do tell us is that talent is not the whole answer. In these examples, its contribution and significance is probably fairly small.

Many personal development books would argue that talent is pretty insignificant, and that practice is the answer. However, I do not believe that can be the whole of the answer either. Practice does not necessarily make perfect. Bad practice certainly doesn't make perfect. I would argue that mediocre practice doesn't make perfect either. Having worked with elite athletes for many years, I don't believe that 10,000 hours of mediocre practice will make anyone world-class.

So, if talent, opportunities and practice do not provide the whole of the answer, what does? What are the factors that differentiate these world-class people from their peers? In the following chapters I will present the key elements that I have found, which bind all of these exceptional people and set them apart from the rest.

Some of the answers may surprise you. Many people imagine that highly successful people are more determined and driven to succeed. Although world-class performers definitely are determined and dedicated, there are also many non world-class people who also display those traits in abundance. Therefore, determination and drive are not differentiators in themselves. If you've read personal development books, you might think that the highest achievers set more goals, or write them down, or create fancy vision boards. However, that's not what I found.

The things that differentiate extreme high achievers are actually quite subtle, but extremely profound. Within this book, we will take a closer look at how ordinary people can achieve extraordinary feats. We will explore how these people think, the decisions that they have made and the way they handle what life has thrown at them. In doing so, we'll start to see exactly what separates these, and other, highly successful people. Often it is their choices and decisions that differentiate highly successful people. They have a different perception and approach challenges differently from the majority of people.

You have an opportunity not only to learn what has made these people stand out, but also to apply the lessons to your own life. These powerful lessons can help us all to shine.

1
Have A Dream

It seems fairly obvious to suggest that high achievers such as those interviewed here, are driven to succeed. But what is it that drives them? Aristotle extolled the virtues of following our dreams and creating our own path in pursuit of happiness. Dreams are incredibly powerful. They help to guide us and motivate us. They provide us with compelling reasons to push ourselves to succeed. However, dreams are not the only reasons to succeed. In studying some of the world's sporting 'Gold Mines', Rasmus Ankersen (2011) discovered that the secret to success is often underpinned by an entirely different motive; need. The drive to succeed for Russian tennis players, Kenyan runners and Korean golfers is often the desire to escape poverty. For these athletes and their families, sporting success provides a route out of material hardship. His discoveries show that often it is the parents of young players that have the greatest desires and the strongest motivation to achieve success. It appears that hunger drives achievement in these instances. In Russia, Kenya and Korea, economic circumstances and the external culture drive an athlete's need for success. However, for many people in the Western world, it's not feasible to create those conditions. In reality, many of us are relatively comfortable, so material hardship and the desire to escape poverty will not be our motivational driver. We cannot reasonably create the environment of poverty that can drive success.

We need something else. We need something that can be equally powerful for us and provide us with a reason that is equally compelling. Interestingly, the world-class people that I interviewed, also have the comforts that come with life in Western society. However, they have found their own compelling reasons! So, what is the motivational force that powers them to reach the very pinnacle of their fields?

A Powerful Dream

Chris Cook dreamt of being an Olympian from an early age.

I have had the dream of becoming an international swimmer since I was very young and it really did fuel my motivation. I think it was probably the first time I saw the Olympics, which would have been 1988. I was nine years old and I saw Adrian Moorehouse win the 100 metres breaststroke. And I just thought, 'wow, that's really cool'. A few months later, they were doing a Speedo promotion thing, him and Nick Gillingham. I went along to the city pool and funnily enough he was there. I remember looking at his medal and thinking, 'I'm alright at breaststroke actually, that's what I want to do'. I wasn't amazing at breaststroke, but it was a stroke that I really enjoyed. It was probably the first time I was aware that I had the dream. It was a very strong feeling.

Obviously, Chris had a strong dream, which was with him since his childhood. However, not everyone has that powerful dream from an early age. Perhaps that's not so unusual. In fact, Chris' experience is atypical of the very successful people I interviewed. Most of them didn't actually conceive of their dreams until much later.

Mountaineer Alan Hinkes didn't contemplate climbing all of the world's 8000-metre peaks when he first started climbing. He has always had his sights set on climbing bigger and more challenging mountains. In fact, Alan Hinkes didn't envisage climbing all 14 of the 8000-metre peaks, until he'd climbed the first eight or so, and was over half way.

The idea of being a World Barista Champion only occurred to James Hoffmann when he met Simon Robertson, who was the UK champion at the time. To James, the idea of being the best in the world seemed fairly abstract, and so he initially focused on trying to achieve the UK title. It was only whilst he was competing that James realized that winning the world title could become a real possibility. As he explained to me, he didn't go to the World Championships with any expectations of winning. In fact, winning the world title took him a little by surprise.

Record-breaking ultra-distance runner Andy McMenemy didn't harbour any genuine ambitions to be a record breaking endurance athlete until well into his 40s. Andy first conceived the idea for 'Challenge 66' whilst he was running the Namibian 24-hour race. He was within 18 kilometres of the finish, having run over 65 miles. As you can imagine, Andy was mentally and physically exhausted and when he stopped for a drink, he quickly realized that he was in a bad way. To distract himself, Andy started to wonder if he could get up the next day and do it again. Having previously read about Dean Karnazes, who ran 50 marathons, in 50 days, in the 50 US states, Andy knew that it must be possible. He asked himself some questions, 'I wonder if I could do that?' 'What would it feel like to achieve it?'. Those questions sparked his curiosity and excitement.

> ## A Dream is Born
>
> Ultra-distance athlete Andy McMenemy described how he first conceived the concept of his 'Challenge 66'.
>
> *Initially I looked at the world record for the number of back-to-back marathons, which stood at 52. Apparently there was a Belgian guy who was contesting that, so I wanted to make sure that my attempt stood a good chance. One night I was talking to my wife Caz, and she said, 'Why don't you do back-to-back ultra-marathons then. Instead of 26 miles a run, simply do 31 miles; it's only an extra five miles a run.' And that's where 'Challenge 66' was born really.*

To many of us the idea of having a dream from childhood, which we then follow through to conclusion, might seem a little far-off. Charles Maher (2005) recognizes that dreams and goals appear at certain points in our life. Some goals come and go. Some dreams are not really dreams at all; they are interesting ideas that we throw around for a while. Those ideas might take us down a few avenues and tempt us to explore them a little further, but are not what we'd describe as 'our dreams'. However, some of them are genuine dreams. They do capture the things that we really want in our lives. They do illustrate what we genuinely want to achieve; they excite us. As Andy

McMenemy told me once over a coffee, when he finds a dream, little sparks of excitement go off. To me, it illustrates a key difference between a dream and a vision.

As I see it, there has to be more than just a vision; more than just our picture of the future. In order to have motivational power, there also has to be emotion. We have to truly connect to that vision as well. It has to be integral to us; a part of us. I'd also argue that there has to be genuine, deep-rooted meaning and purpose. This is a principle that is echoed by psychologists such as Rollo May and Viktor Frankl. Throughout the course of our own lives, we will no doubt have appreciated the motivational power that comes with *purpose*. When we have a purpose, we tend to be able to achieve a lot more.

Dreaming is not Enough!

Having a dream may not be enough on its own. Daft as it sounds, many people have dreams but don't follow them. It's true. Many of us don't follow our dreams. Why not? Well, we might think our dreams are silly. We might not believe they are possible. Our dreams might not fit in with everyone else's expectations or plans for us. We might actually compromise our dreams for other people.

A friend of mine, who was an aspiring entrepreneur, once said to me, 'I don't think I have a dream'. This intrigued me so I started discussing it with him a little more. When we got a little deeper, it became apparent that he had many dreams and ambitions, but that he'd never given them any real recognition. He'd never seen them as *a dream* because he'd viewed them as a bit outlandish. They weren't very realistic. They were not easily achievable, so he'd assigned them to the junk pile. He hadn't honoured them, recognized them and nurtured them. He'd never given them any energy. He'd never genuinely tried to realize them. Instead, he'd ignored them because he felt they were daft. Ironically, the things he spent his time pursuing were unrelated to his dreams. They were much more realistic but he wasn't genuinely passionate about them. They were simply a means to an end. Consequently he flitted from one thing to another and never spent very long on any one project. His motivation petered out when he failed to realize the success he was looking for after a few months. His motivation was entirely tied to the outcome. If the project didn't make money quickly, there wasn't any point in it. He was not engaged in the project for its own sake or because he believed in it.

I believe that everybody dreams. The difference between those who follow their dreams, and those who don't, comes down to whether the dreams are honoured, recognized and nurtured. Without recognition and energy, our dreams will wither. If we give them recognition and energy, they will become strong and vibrant.

It's possible that our dreams have a companion that is equally (or potentially even more) powerful. That companion is **passion**! Those who really stand out have an absolute intrinsic love for what they do. They are incredibly passionate and they understand how important that passion has been in driving their success. Centre for Life Chief Executive Linda Conlon understands that success requires more than just great ideas. She understands that ideas are easy. Bringing great ideas to life requires much more. She knows that the tenacity and energy required, comes from passion. To create the Centre for Life, her team needed to think big, have an exciting vision and have absolute belief in it.

"Passion is more important than skills in making things happen. You need to think big and have the vision and the belief to keep going."

Linda Conlon, Centre for Life Chief Executive

An All Consuming Passion

Alan Hinkes understands that climbing has always been a passion, and therefore, an integral part of his life:

People often ask if mountaineering was a hobby. I hate that word 'hobby', it sounds like stamp collecting. To me, mountaineering is not even a pastime. Right from the start it is something I had a passion for. I would never have called it a hobby, it was always beyond that. It was always my life. It's funny, journalists always write, 'former teacher, Alan Hinkes', which suggests that at one point I was a teacher and then I became a climber. I was always a climber, way before I was a teacher. Nowadays I do make my living from climbing. But to say former teacher is like saying 'former child'.

This level of devotion to a particular field is echoed by others. Kenny Atkinson starts in the kitchen at 6.30am, works until late afternoon and then comes back in to run the evening shift. Normally he'll finish his working day at midnight. It might sound like a gruelling schedule to most of us but it doesn't fluster Kenny. He explained that he loves delivering 40 to 50 covers, knowing that the customers have had a tremendous experience. As a result, he is able to bounce back into the kitchen first thing the following morning, fresh and enthused. He does that day after day, year on year. Clearly, passion is at the heart of Kenny's success.

A Strong Reason

The strength of this reason and purpose is tested in the journey to become the best you can be. We are presented with many choices which could potentially pull us away from the path to achieving our potential. The choices we make, ultimately have an enormous influence on our success. Bruce Duncan's passion for adventure racing actually shaped a number of pivotal life decisions, including his choice of university and his career path. From a young age, Bruce wanted to compete at the World Orienteering Championship. When he chose to study Chemical Engineering, he made a conscious decision to study this at Edinburgh University because it was the best for orienteering and had the best orienteering club in the country. As Bruce studied Chemical Engineering, he found that it simply didn't give him enough time for orienteering. Therefore Bruce changed his course to Geology, which allowed him to increase his training and compete at a higher level.

Polar explorer Ben Saunders made similar decisions to follow his passion ahead of the more 'sensible' or conventional options. As a fan of adventure, Ben thought that the Army seemed like an obvious career option. Although he didn't have a degree, Ben was enrolled in the Army officer training programme at Sandhurst (Military Academy). However, after 11 months, he left of his own accord after realizing that he valued his freedom. A few years earlier, Ben had taken a year out to trek in the Himalayas and then worked with John Ridgway (the first person to row across the Atlantic) at his School of Adventure in Scotland. Ben described how John Ridgway would challenge him by asking 'Why not? Why don't you have a go?'. Perhaps these questions underpinned Ben's decision to abandon the 'solid and sensible' career option and follow his passion.

For Bruce, orienteering was foremost in his life. He put his passion for orienteering first, and made sure that his education and subsequent career choices fitted around it. Alan and Ben chose careers in mountaineering and polar expedition, ahead of professions in teaching or the Army. Interestingly, one of the words most associated with highly successful people, is *sacrifice*. They have often made tough choices to sacrifice certain things in order to progress in their chosen discipline. They have made the choices which others have not made.

Double Olympian Chris Cook had some tough choices to make at a fairly tender age. He noticed that his friends began to disappear from the sport at the age of 14 or 15. At one point he looked around and noticed that he was the only one left from his group of friends. Chris had to make a choice, to fit in with his group of friends or remain in swimming. It's a tough decision at an age when most people are desperately trying to fit in and belong. At that time Chris was not a particularly good swimmer; he hadn't even made a national final. As his career progressed, these challenges came around on a regular basis. In his mid- to late-20s, Chris trained alongside teenagers. At that time, many of his friends were starting careers and earning a good living as professional people such as accountants and lawyers. He would often ask himself whether he had made the right choice, or whether he was just carrying on because it was what he'd always done. Chris' passion for swimming kept him going and ultimately contributed to his undoubted success.

The Decision to be Great

Kenny Atkinson explains how he used his holiday time when he was a junior chef in order to become better.

When I knew I wanted to be a chef I said, 'if I am going to be a chef, I want to be a great chef'. I had two weeks holiday from work and I wanted to get some experience working in a Michelin starred restaurant, because that's what I wanted to be. The chef there said to me, 'be a sponge, don't ask about salary, don't ask about hours, just try to soak up as much knowledge as possible'. He told me that I'd forget more than I learned and to write everything down. To this day, I still have little notebooks from every restaurant I've worked in. I have recipes, drawings and sketches because you forget these things. And that's what I did.

I was being paid £35 a week for doing a 60-hour week at work, and I had to pay £5 a week board to my mother, which I wasn't happy about. So I was getting £30 per week, and I did that for two years. But I knew at that time, when I saw the likes of Marco Pierre-White, the Roux brothers and Gary Rhodes; this is what I wanted to be.

You have to make loads of sacrifices. You have to work long hours for little pay at the start. It's hard when everyone around you is earning good money and has a social life and you don't. In a few jobs I slept on the floor at the restaurant so that I could finish the shift at midnight and be in again first thing.

Interestingly, high achievers recognize that although they make sacrifices, their choices are positive. They are choosing to do the thing they love, whilst realizing that it means they'll have to miss out on something else. Adventure racer Bruce Duncan commented on this point at the first Be World-Class Conference in October 2011. He understands that by choosing to dedicate himself to adventure racing, he's missed out on a lot of other things. He's chosen adventure racing over a 'normal' lifestyle, with its socializing, parties and nights out. Bruce also knows that as a consequence, he isn't as close to many of his friends as he could be. However, Bruce is aware that dedicating himself to adventure racing was a positive choice, and that there is a tremendous up-side. Bruce loves being in the wilderness and discovering wild places. Adventure racing has given him some amazing experiences and allowed him to travel the world, doing what he loves. Which do you think Bruce would rather do, go out partying or race through an unspoilt wilderness?

"I have loved doing everything I have done, so it doesn't seem like a sacrifice."

**Bruce Duncan, Team GB captain and
world-leading adventure racer**

The Power of Passion

Passion, and a love for what you do, seem to be fundamental to these very successful people. But what difference does passion actually make? Let's start by remembering that expert performance develops over many years and requires many thousands of hours of deliberate practice. Geoff Colvin (2008), recognizes that 'deliberate practice', by its very nature, is not always particularly enjoyable. It is hard work. It can be frustrating. When we engage in deliberate practice we make mistakes and fail. Therefore, it requires a great deal of dedication. Many of the world-leading people I interviewed would agree that it took them at least ten years to become expert in their field. When we consider these points again, it becomes obvious that those with passion, are far better equipped to embark on, and enjoy the journey to become the best in their field. Their intrinsic love for what they do is powerful. They are not in it purely for the outcome, the destination, or the rewards. There is psychological research and theory that support these ideas. Robert Vallerand (2008), explains that harmonious passion leads people to choose and engage in activities that they love. When people engage in activities they love, they are able to dedicate themselves to them completely. In doing so, they stand a much greater chance of developing genuine expertise and performing at a high level. Motivation that is intrinsic and based on a love and passion for the task, is often considered to be stronger, more stable and enduring. Therefore, a harmonious passion and intrinsic motivation are often found in those who have reached the pinnacle of their discipline.

"I find that when I have a passion for something, I put my whole heart and soul into it"
Kenny Atkinson, twice Michelin-starred chef

Alan Hinkes told me how a love for the mountain is a key component to being a successful mountaineer. He explained that if you want to climb a mountain, you have got to want to be there. Those who don't love being on a mountain will often become impatient. They will either 'bail out' in his words, or make a bid for the summit too soon. To be successful, you need to wait for the ideal weather and conditions. Sometimes this requires a mountaineer to stay at base camp for a few weeks. Alan recognizes that it's uncomfortable. It means living in a tent, in sub-zero temperatures, eating the mountaineer's rations. For Alan, waiting for the perfect conditions is no problem, even if it means being on a mountain for a few weeks, because there is nowhere he'd rather be.

Passion vs Need

As we have discussed, there are a variety of powerful motivators. An intrinsic love and passion is just one. So, is *the* reason important, or is it enough simply to have a strong reason? Let's compare the accounts of the world-class winners interviewed here with former world number one tennis player Marat Safin a product of the hugely successful Russian tennis system. His motivation was driven by his parents' desire to make a better life through tennis, rather than an intrinsic love for the sport. At age 19, Marat won the US Open. Along with this prestigious Grand Slam victory came fame, financial fortune and fast cars. Interestingly, the following few years were quite turbulent for young Marat. He struggled to maintain his form and became more famous for his temper than his tennis. What had changed? Arguably, he was no longer powered by the same need that had driven him to success. He now had the material comforts that he'd strived so long to gain. Perhaps his reason had disappeared.

Marat Safin is not alone. In his study of sporting 'Gold Mines', Rasmus Ankersen (2011), also spent time in the favelas of Rio de Janeiro, birthplace of many Brazilian football greats. He found that the boys of the favelas were also looking for an escape through football. Many Brazilian players view football as a means of becoming rich and creating their dream life. That is their reason. It drives them to work incredibly hard. However, once they have achieved that dream, and created the lifestyle, there is no reason to work hard. Perhaps it is no surprise that many highly acclaimed Brazilian players have very short careers at the top level (perhaps just a handful of seasons), before they dip.

So, having *the right* reason arguably provides much more sustainable and enduring motivation. It allows you to remain at the pinnacle, rather than just reach it. Perhaps, it goes further than that. Mountaineer Alan Hinkes explains that having the right reason not only makes the difference between success and failure, but also life and death. Experience tells him that the vast majority of people who attempt all fourteen 8000-metre peaks don't survive. He's also noticed that they usually get killed on the twelfth, thirteenth or final ascent. It is not because those peaks are technically more challenging. The reason is because they start to 'push the envelope that bit more'. He understands that the lure of prestige, recognition, fame and fortune, can entice people to change their decision making and take more risks. According to Alan Hinkes, no French climbers have climbed all of the 8000-metre peaks because they would be as famous in France as David Beckham is in the UK. Alan didn't have the same lure. His reason was simple – he did it because he *wanted* to do it.

What's Your Reason?

To be motivated, we need a compelling reason. In order to master our motivation, we need to be acutely aware of this reason. It has to be meaningful. We really have to want it! Often though, we forget the reason. It slips to the back of our mind. We start doing things out of habit. Sometimes we confuse our reasons. Sometimes our reasons change over time. We might start a business for the love of doing it and because we know the value it gives to others. Over time, we may lose sight of this and become embroiled in the day to day grind of finances, HR issues and red tape. Equally, our reasons might start to distort. We forget about our love for the business and the value we give. We might start seeing the business as a means of gaining recognition and respect from others. It becomes our way of making our fortune; a way of getting the big house and flashy car.

Many athletes also find that their motives change over time. When they start out, their motive is simple. They love playing. Their motivation is simply driven by love and enjoyment for what they do. However for many, that picture changes. After a while, another agenda appears. The sport starts to give them other things. Winning gives them something new. When they achieve positive results they begin to gain recognition and respect from others. For a young athlete, this can start to become the primary motive. The sport then becomes a vehicle to achieve success and recognition. Their reason starts to evolve and becomes orientated around winning. A lot of coaches might see this as a good thing. Shouldn't athletes be motivated and driven to win? Isn't that the point? Surely the athletes that are motivated by winning are the ones who are most likely to be successful. They have a hunger and a desire for success that drives them.

In reality, it can be a double-edged sword. What if the athlete is not experiencing success? What if they are not winning? If their reason for participating is to win, the reason could well disappear. If that happens, motivation will evaporate very quickly. I've known many athletes to quit their sport because they hit a tough patch. Their motivation wasn't robust and couldn't carry them through. The irony is that they will say they quit because they weren't enjoying it any more. What they really mean is that their enjoyment was tied to winning. When the success dried up, so did the enjoyment and the motivation. A few years ago, I worked with an international swimmer who found exactly that. When success and recognition dried up, her reasons to compete evaporated with them.

Are you genuinely motivated by the love of what you do, or has your reason started to evolve? Often the best way to find out, is to see how you feel in the absence of a reason. For example, if you took away winning, would that seriously knock your motivation? If you didn't have the social interaction of your team-mates, would that dent it? What if no-one gave you praise or recognition? Would you still be as motivated? Those are often the acid tests.

In order to have strong motivation, we need a reason that is strong, robust, enduring and compelling. Psychologists Edward Deci and Richard Ryan (2002) found that motivation that comes from within is more stable and more likely to last, than motivation that is driven by external rewards or recognition. It really is very simple; you have to really want it. You can't make yourself want something because someone else wants you to have it. You will never be truly motivated by the need to please other people. Your motivation has to be genuine and has to come from within. It is not a coincidence that many truly great people have been inspired by their dreams. When they are interviewed, they often talk about the fact that they've been following their dreams. Our passion, love and dreams are powerful and enduring motives. They are authentic. They are ours.

So how do you know what your reasons are? If your reason to be in business is to make a lot of money, gain recognition and drive the flashy car, you will find that your motivation takes a nose dive if you're struggling financially. If you are motivated because of a love for what you do and because you know that what you do has value, your motivation will tend not to be knocked as much if you hit financial struggles.

Understanding the reason is the foundation to mastering motivation. Motivating a team requires us not only to understand our own reasons, but also those of the team members. Are they at work purely for the money? Is it because they enjoy being part of the team? Are they here to be successful and to be recognized? Do they get satisfaction from achieving? Or do they simply love doing the job? Everyone is different. Most people have multiple reasons, but will normally have one or two that are stronger than others. When we understand those more fully, motivating the team becomes easier. Many managers try to inject their reasons into other people. It may have some short-term impact, but doesn't normally work in the long-term.

In business and sport, motivating yourself and your team has an enormous impact on performance. When lack of motivation becomes an issue, people often start to take their foot off the gas or lose their discipline. They start choosing to do the easier things rather than the difficult things. They don't push themselves quite as hard. They get despondent quicker. Rather than sticking with something until they make it work, they might try a few times but give up because they think 'it's just not working'. They shy away from the really tough challenges and stick to their comfort zone more closely. If there is a choice to do something now or postpone it, they start to postpone. The end result is a negative downward spiral of reducing performance, reducing confidence and reducing motivation. Ultimately of course, the results suffer!

What if your reason was simple? What if you were passionate about what you did?

Aligning Dreams and Passion

Ironically, a few years ago I found myself struggling because I had dropped my passion, and started focusing on the money.

Coaching is my passion. It's what I believe I am on this planet to do; it's my purpose. However, since I was a kid, I have always dreamed of being a millionaire businessman. When I was offered an opportunity, which I thought would help me fulfil my dreams and make me my millions, I went for it. Instead of following my passion, I started focusing on the money. To cut a long story short, the opportunity didn't work out, no matter how many hours I put into it. One Sunday morning I sat down with my wife. I was frustrated because the hard work had not paid off. We were almost broke and I couldn't work out where it had all gone wrong. I remember saying to her, 'Maybe I am just supposed to be a coach. After all, it's what I love and it's what I am good at.' Her response . . . 'Why can't you make your millions by being a coach; instead of trying to *either* make your millions, *or* be a coach?' Perhaps I didn't believe that being a coach could make millions? At that point I realized that I'd dropped my passion in pursuit of the money. As I sit here writing this chapter, I can tell you I am not a millionaire, but I am passionate! It doesn't mean that I have dropped my dream and given up on being a millionaire! That is still my dream. Now though, my dream is aligned with my passion, not in competition with it.

The Power of Love

So having a passion and intrinsic love for what you do, is what gives us the motivational fuel required for the journey. If the journey to become a genuine expert is likely to take over ten years and take many thousands of hours, you can bet there will be a few challenges along the way. Twice-Michelin starred chef Kenny Atkinson described his journey as 'a roller coaster', full of ups and downs, hurdles and challenges. Passion is there-fore vital to help us keep going through the challenges. For Kenny, the buzz comes from working in the kitchen with fresh ingredients and making great food. The fact that every day is different, with the possibility of seeing things he's never seen before and learning new things, is what fuels his passion. As Kenny says, 'I just love it. I really love it.'

When successful people hit challenges, they don't seem to dust themselves off and get back up again. Instead, they bounce back up. Their motivation and enthusiasm doesn't seem to wane if things go wrong or if they've not achieved their desired outcome quickly. Their love for what they do is intrinsic. Doing what they do seems to be more important than the outcome.

"Coming back is the success and the summit is a bonus, that's what I always say."
Alan Hinkes, world-leading mountaineer

"Nearly six months on and I still haven't filled in the paperwork for the Guinness World Record submission. It is 180-odd pages. It's still in the cupboard. I've completed the challenge, so what's a certificate on the wall?"
Andy McMenemy, record-breaking ultra-distance runner, on completing 'Challenge 66'

I'm sure that completing 180 pages of paper work is far less demanding than running 66 consecutive ultra-marathons! However for Andy, the reason to complete the paperwork is not as great as the reason to complete the challenge. In the Introduction, England Squash's National Head Coach Chris Robertson identified that many talented, young squash players give up when they hit challenges. As we will see in the coming chapters, those who reach the very pinnacle of their field constantly encounter challenges. All of them have failed and continue to fail when they push themselves to their limits. Their dreams and their passion give them the ability to keep pushing and keep failing. Success is not the reason to do what they do. Doing it is reason enough, so success is a bonus. Therefore, they are willing to try and fail. Their journeys have taken years and are comprised of many thousands of hours of dedication. Their journeys are made up of thousands of steps, and it is their passion, that has continually given them the motivation to take the next step.

Summary

- There are many different reasons and motives that drive people to become the best they can be, including hunger for success and need.
- Dreams, passion and intrinsic love for what you do give you compelling, stable, robust and enduring motivation.
- By comparison, extrinsic motives can run out of steam or fall at the tougher hurdles.
- There may be times where you need to be prepared to make tough choices, to follow your passion ahead of more 'sensible' options.
- This strong passion allows you to make sacrifices, whilst at the same time, knowing that they are in fact positive choices.

2
Focus On The Next Step

We know how important it is to have a compelling vision and a dream. No doubt there is a great deal of wisdom in the words, 'start with the end in mind'. Of course, we need to know where we are going. However, high achievers seem to understand the need to constantly keep their focus on the next step.

> *"Good navigation helps you move twice as quickly . . . you have to have a long-term goal, the destination, but it is all about how you get there. There is no point in thinking beyond the stage you are on."*
>
> **Bruce Duncan, Team GB captain**
> **and world-leading adventure racer**

In navigation, focusing on the next step may seem like an obvious and crucial point, and it's a great analogy for performance in all walks of life. But how does this apply to organizations that are growing and navigating their own challenges? Polar explorer Ben Saunders knows that his challenge extends beyond trekking and navigating in the Arctic. He needs to raise funds and manage a project before he even steps onto the ice. Ben understands how important it is to focus on the next step in both environments.

> *"The ultimate goal can seem so abstract that it seems hard to achieve, daunting. I remember thinking numerous times,*

'maybe today's the day I quit', because the challenge just looked too big. The only way to deal with it is to take one step at a time. That's how I have approached everything. That's how it's all been achieved. What's the next thing, the thing I do right now? Is it taking me in the right direction?"
Ben Saunders, record-breaking polar explorer

Ben's thoughts are echoed by Linda Conlon, Centre for Life Chief Executive. She understands that her team are also engaged in a journey that is taken one step at a time. She explained that there are many different stages in the growth and development of an organization. Each stage requires a different set of skills. For example, the skills to make things happen are different from the skills needed to keep them happening. Linda ensures that her team focus on the needs of each moment.

"Although we need an eye on the strategy and the direction, we can't afford to take our eye off of the 'here and now'."
Linda Conlon, Centre for Life Chief Executive

Keir Worth recognizes the same challenges in keeping England Squash at the top of the world. As the Head of Performance, it is his role to understand the vision and strategy. Keir also emphasizes the need to remain focused on the 'here and now' and to know what the next step is. He described the way in which they constantly assess how the things they do each day, feed into their vision for the future. Keir is also aware that their success tomorrow is determined by the things they do today. Equally, if they are struggling today, it is likely to stem from something they did in the past. He will ask his team what they did six months ago that caused them the issues.

Strategy, Tactics and Execution

Both Keir and Linda understand the difference between strategic focus, tactical focus and execution. Within an organization, there are normally a variety of roles. Some focus on strategy and direction, others focus on tactical implementation, whilst some people are responsible for delivery. However, at some level, all of us have responsibilities in all three areas. Even those who are strategists need to ensure they understand their own tactics and can deliver their job well. In fact, our focus on strategy, tactics and execution must constantly shift in order for us to perform. Professor Frank Bond (2006) refers to our ability to focus on the present moment whilst pursuing our end goal, as 'psychological flexibility'. His research suggests that these abilities are crucial to both mental health and performance. This concept is closely aligned with the findings from management research (Collins and Hansen, 2011), which suggest that highly successful business leaders have the ability to zoom out (in order to see the strategic picture and take strategic decisions) and then zoom back in, in order to execute their strategy. This enables successful operators to deliver their game plan, whilst being able to respond to unforeseen events, as well as having the ability to focus on the right things at the right times.

Extreme Focus

Mountaineer Alan Hinkes understands that being able to focus in the moment is a life-saving skill.

When I came off the summit of Kanchenjunga, I thought I had had it. I honestly thought I was going to die. In that situation, I had to think tactically not strategically. There was nothing I could do about the strategic picture. There was nothing I could do about the avalanche potential; the snow I was on that could avalanche me to my death. There was

> *nothing I could do about that. The first rule of avoiding avalanches is not to go out during, or 24 hours after, a snow fall. I was in a blizzard and there was nothing I could do about that. I was over 8000 metres up. If I stayed where I was, I was dead. I just had to fight through it. So that strategic picture had to be pushed right out so that the fear and anxiety didn't overwhelm me. The task in hand was simply to get down and not to fall. I just had to simply find the route and focus on that. And it became pure pleasure. I guess I started putting things in boxes and took them one at a time, literally one step at a time. I just had to think of the task in smaller chunks.*
>
> *Right now I am focused on getting my kit ready for Everest because I have to, and there is a cut-off point. Once I've done that I can really start to think about the next thing. Then it will be getting to Kathmandu and getting the kit together there. When we leave Kathmandu we will be trekking for 10–12 days to get acclimatized and get fit so we will focus entirely on that.*
>
> *There is no point in thinking any further ahead. There is no point in thinking about the mountain at this point and what could happen, just think about the task in hand, with the bigger picture in the back of your mind.*

The Answer is Right in Front of You!

These highly successful people are all presenting a very consistent message. Their success is due in part to their ability to focus on what is in front of them. They are aware of the bigger picture, but their focus is honed onto the task in hand. At the moment, I am working with a motor racing driver. He knows that in order to be successful, he needs to hone his focus to specific cues and then rapidly shift his focus onto the next. He describes that when he's coming into a corner, he will be watching for the breaking point. Then, he'll switch focus to the apex of the corner as he turns. When he's coming out of the turn, he'll listen to the revs picking up as he exits the corner, and then he'll start to feel the steering as he transitions from the corner to the straight. He also talks about feeling the G-forces and feeling himself holding his body position to counteract them. This process absolutely requires him to focus moment by moment on the critical things that will help him drive his car as fast as possible.

These principles apply equally to business. In my executive coaching work, I encourage people to focus on their next step, and not to get too far ahead of themselves. Recently I have been working with a Managing Director, to help him improve some of the key processes within his business. In one area, he has rated his current performance as a 5/10. He knows what a 10/10 looks like, but is less clear about what a 6/10 looks like. In reality, he'll only get close to 10/10 by first achieving 6/10, then 7/10, then 8/10. His first task is to focus on getting from 5/10 to 6/10. If he can start to identify 'the niggles' and frustrations he currently has, and focus on ironing those out, he'll actually start working his way from a 5/10 to a 6/10 and beyond. That way, it all has a very tangible impact. When we do this, we start to understand what we need to do today!

Commonwealth Champion Chris Cook found it difficult to get his head around the four-year Olympic cycle. He needed to break it down and understand the opportunities that lay right in front of him. Although he would have targets for the training cycle or training year, he would focus completely on each training session. Chris understood that he needed to squeeze every ounce of possible benefit from each session. He would often start a session by asking 'how is this hour going to help me swim two lengths of the pool quicker'.

> *"Every day you get a bag load of opportunities to grow and develop and take steps towards your goal."*
> **Chris Cook, double Olympian and Commonwealth champion**

I've seen that mind-set separates athletes. I have seen squads of swimmers all pick up the same training card when they walk into the pool hall. Some will follow the training card, but they won't focus fully on every component. They might be a bit sloppy in their technique. They might not nail every turn. When the coach tells them to swim at 100%, they may do 93% instead. However, the swimmer next to them might apply themselves fully to every stroke, every turn and every length. They'll pay attention to their rhythm and breathing, their push off the wall and the feel as they catch the water. The athletes who have that mind-set might only get 0.1% better today, but they will get another 0.1% better tomorrow and another 0.1% the next day. If you look at these athletes in a year's time, there is a slight difference. If you look at them in two years' time, there is a discernible difference. The gap between one athlete and the next often arises because of the way they approach that individual session.

Do World-Class People Set Goals?

In reality, many of the great athletes I've worked with don't seem to set formal, structured goals. The accounts of these world-class performers indicate that their approach is similar. Of course, they all know what they want to achieve, but I have not seen evidence that they follow a structured goal setting process. There don't appear to be any formal three-year plans or five-year plans, or SMARTER goals. There are no grand mission statements or fancy vision boards. Instead, their goals seem to be a lot more immediate, and also more fluid.

Fluid Goals

England International squash player Alison Waters has found similar challenges as she's navigated her way through injury and back to fitness.

> It's been a tricky one for me whilst I've been injured. You want to set targets for when you think you'll be back but you're not in control of whether you'll achieve them. I was supposed to play a tournament, and had entered for the end of January, thinking I might be fine. Now I am realizing that it's out of the question and I will set my sights on the National Championships. Even that isn't for sure, so you have to keep setting realistic little targets and working on them. The last thing I want to do is rush it, having been off three or four months. I don't want to rush it to get back for a tournament. For the sake of a week or two, I could save myself another three or four months on the treatment table. I think you need to keep being realistic and keep working step by step.

In fact, during the first Be World-Class Conference, Keir Worth explained how England Squash use this approach. He describes the process as 'tacking'. Just as the skipper of a yacht knows the direction he wants to go (and the destination he's aiming for), he also knows that it is not a direct route from A to B. To reach his destination, he'll need to 'tack', as he responds to changes in the wind and the water conditions. It is a discipline that requires the skipper and his crew to be in the 'here and now'!

Be in 'the Moment'

Keeping our focus in the moment is a key component of peak performance. Peak performances and peak experiences are often described by a number of different terms. You may have heard people refer to The Zone or to a Flow State. Essentially these terms refer to the same phenomenon. They describe a state of complete concentration and total absorption. People often report that peak performances seem effortless. They seem to have more time, see things more clearly and find the performance easy. Some have described feeling like they have a Midas touch. Everything they attempt seems to come off.

Psychologist Professor Mihaly Csikszentmihalyi (1990) has researched Flow States extensively. His research tells us that these peak performance states share a number of consistent features. The Zone is a state in which we are completely involved in an activity for its own sake. We lose ourselves in the task. We become immersed. Simply doing the activity becomes its own reward. Psychologists term this as *optimal intrinsic motivation*. It refers to a state where our whole being is involved in the task. We are so focused on the activity that we have almost no way of being distracted. There is no spare attention for anything else. In fact, there is probably not enough attention to even focus on ourselves.

Performing at our peak is fundamental if we aspire to be the best we can be. If we can't perform consistently well, we're never going to truly shine. If we aren't able to focus our attention, we will struggle to perform at our peak. As the accounts from these highly acclaimed performers show; focus is essential. As you may also know from your own experience, honing and controlling your focus can be a challenge.

Interestingly, James Clash (2003), a writer and adventurer, explains that when climbing the world's highest mountains, a climber may sometimes have to take six to eight breaths per step when at altitude. That level of disciplined focus represents an enormous mental demand.

> *"I'd often make sure that I wriggled my toes on every step to keep them moving and warm. Step, scrunch, scrunch, step, scrunch, scrunch . . . you can't do it semi-automatically, you really have to* think *to do it."*
> **Alan Hinkes, world-leading mountaineer, on the focus and effort required to avoid getting frost-bite**

That level of focus demands that we are fully engaged with *the moment*. This is a concept that is widely advocated for success in life, spiritual development, sports coaching and sports performance. England Squash's National Head Coach Chris Robertson also appreciates the importance of being in the moment. He recognizes that in the game of squash, there is a constant shift of focus between perception, decision and action. It is this cycle (known as the PDA cycle) that links awareness, tactics, decision making, movement and technical execution in the game.

Chris describes how world-class players are able to hone their focus on each step and how this allows them to play great shots.

Squash is an incredibly fast-paced game. To the onlooker, it can appear to be little more than a blur. Chris Robertson understands that within a game of squash there are very brief moments of 'quiet time', when players can focus purely on playing the shot. Through his coaching, Chris emphasizes the need for players to develop 'shot responsibility' in those moments. Once the player has executed the shot, they must switch focus back onto the perceptual and decision-making elements of the game. The ability to rapidly switch focus onto an appropriate cue is a crucial skill for an elite squash player. Chris' aim, when working with players, is to allow them to feel as if they have an eternity when they play their shot. He understands the importance of protecting that 'quiet time' which allows players to absolutely immerse themselves in the moment.

There are parallels between the focus required in squash and many other areas of life. Our ability to focus on the key moments, and switch our focus onto what is important *right now*, is something that is consistent in great performers. This focus helps us see opportunities and threats. It helps us make the best possible decisions.

Tackling the Challenge One Moment at a Time

Retired US Navy SEAL Gary Rossi also understands the importance of focusing on each step. It was a key feature to his success in Special Forces operations, and also something that he applies to sports coaching and business consultancy now.

If you have a mission, break the mission up into little goals so that you can achieve what you set out to do. In the SEALs, we all have to go through

> *Prisoner Of War (POW) training. Before we deploy, we are put through SERE school – Search Evasion Resistance and Escape. As a POW, you can't plan a particular period of time, because you have no idea how long it will take. But you have got to take hour by hour, minute by minute and keep your mind focused on the little things. As a management consultant, there is a saying that you can't eat the elephant all at once, you have to take a little bite at a time. You have to break the whole down into little pieces and focus on each one to achieve those goals.*

Through his consultancy work with businesses, and through coaching a soccer team in the US, Gary also knows how these principles translate into sport and business.

> *It's the same with the soccer team. I often have a challenge keeping them focused on our team and our games, because they have competitive games for their clubs outside of high school. At the moment their minds are on their club games and their national cup. I often stop them and bring them back to the game here and now. I need to keep them on task. I do not want to hear about national cup or state cup. Those things are a distraction. Those things draw our focus from the task in hand.*

Fall in Love With the Process

So why is it that these people are able to focus on the next step, whilst other people find their focus drifting off into the future or dwelling on the past? Perhaps we have already uncovered part of the answer. Maybe these very high achievers are able to focus on the moment because they have an intrinsic love of it. Their passion and love for what they do allows them to immerse themselves fully in each moment. It is difficult to immerse yourself in something that you don't enjoy. Our natural reaction is to try to escape what we're doing, rather than becoming absorbed by it. It's far easier to become immersed in something we are interested by, fascinated by, or have a genuine love for.

When listening to these world-class people, I notice that their enjoyment isn't restricted to achieving the end goal. They are not tied to the outcome or focused purely on the result. Anyone that is tied to the result, the outcome or the success, is likely to be focused on the future. They are likely to find themselves either dreaming of the future, or worrying about it. Whichever they do, they will not be present; they will not be in the moment. Their accounts clearly show that although they have dreams and ambitions, success is not their only driver. Arguably, it is not the primary motive either.

All Journeys are Taken one Step at a Time

In reality, we can often only see the next step or two along our journey. Although we might like to plan many steps into the future, our future can never be completely predictable. We need to be able to adapt and remain agile. The experiences of our own journey will also tell us that we often develop the skills that we need for each stage as we go along. When we embark on new challenges, it's rare that we know each step that we will encounter along the way. Normally, we don't have all the answers in advance or all of the skills required when we take those first steps. This is especially true when we're entering new territory and pushing the boundaries.

Polar explorer Ben Saunders understands this acutely. He and his team have taken on many challenges that have never been attempted before. The most recent is a record-breaking Antarctic expedition. Ben knows that often, there simply are no answers.

"I don't know how we'll do it. We're taking on challenges we've never taken on before. I don't have the answers but I do know the reason. If everyone else knows the reason, generally they respond when I ask them 'how'."
Ben Saunders, record-breaking polar explorer

As the Chinese proverb says, 'a journey of a thousand miles starts with a single step'. I actually believe there is more to it than that. A journey of a thousand miles is entirely composed of single steps. Although walking a thousand miles might seem daunting, in reality it is just a series of very achievable steps. This is a philosophy that can be seen in many remarkable personal journeys and is central to the success of great athletes and high achievers, like record-breaking ultra-distance runner Andy McMenemy. Over coffee, Andy told me that 'Challenge 66' simply required him to take 3.3 million individual strides. Although it seems like a daunting number, he knew that each stride had to be taken one at a time. Therefore, Andy broke the challenge into smaller chunks. He would literally focus on each day, and sometimes each 400-metre lap that he was running. Andy viewed each ultra-marathon as a working day with six to eight hours of physical work, plus the nutrition, rest and recovery routines. He knew the importance of every stage of the process. Therefore his strategy was simply to repeat this 66 times.

"Each stage is incredibly important, so you have to get it right. If I didn't go through the process, it had a big knock on effect

to my energy and mood. That's when I started to think 'can I go on?'."

Andy McMenemy, record-breaking ultra-distance runner

That same mentality can be applied across years as well. Olympic swimmer Chris Cook and I discussed how the 'meteoric rise' that people sometimes perceive is actually an illusion. Far from being a sudden event, Chris' appearance on the world stage was an accumulation of many steps. The idea that he suddenly just appeared on the world stage is absolutely not true. I think of it a bit like an iceberg. Many people only see the tip that pokes above the surface. They don't see the vast majority under the surface. Chris didn't burst onto the world stage at all. There were years of work before he even got his first international call-up. Even then it wasn't all it first seemed. After receiving a letter from the official GB team inviting him to compete for his country, Chris excitedly told his friends, family and the local press. To his dismay this letter was followed by a second, a few weeks later. The second letter explained that there had been an administration error and that Chris was not going to be included in the squad.

"It was awful. And I knew there and then that if I wanted to stick this out, there was going to be plenty of challenges, a lot of soul searching and a lot of lessons to learn."

Chris Cook, double Olympian and Commonwealth champion, describes his reaction to the news

Twice Michelin-starred chef Kenny Atkinson's journey also shows that there are many years of focused work before the recognition. Fairly early on in that journey, he made the decision to be the best chef he could be. Kenny started by knocking on the doors of the best restaurants in his home town of

Newcastle. He told the head chef he wanted to be a commis chef (junior chef), and eventually got a job. When the head chef left to take a job in the south, Kenny asked if he could join him. After a while, Kenny started to realize that there was more to learn, so he applied to do an unpaid two-week working trial at a Michelin-starred restaurant called The Mandarin Oriental in London. He remembers the head chef telling him, "Be a sponge, work hard, don't ask about the pay, watch and listen." Through this experience, Kenny learned many of the disciplines required to make it to the top. As well as learning about food and ingredients, he learned not to compromise his standards. However, after taking a head chef's position of his own, he still had to work ridiculous hours for several years, before earning his first Michelin star. Today, Kenny is a very well-respected and high profile chef, who has also won an array of awards and accolades.

Kenny's story is another great example of a journey that was taken one step at a time, and over the course of many years. As with the other accounts we've seen, it highlights the importance of taking consistent steps in the right direction. Jim Collins (2011) noticed a similar pattern in the way highly successful organizations developed. He coined the term '20 Mile Marching', after noticing that successful organizations take consistent, but often modest advances towards their goal, rather than huge leaps.

Imagine a builder, building a staircase. If the builder is focused on getting the staircase finished as quickly as possible, it's unlikely that they will dedicate themselves completely to each individual step. If short-cuts have been made on any of the steps, it's likely that the staircase will not be 100%. Do you fancy walking up that staircase? Personally, I'd prefer to know that each step of that staircase was properly constructed. I would want to know that focus, care and attention had been given to the creation of each individual step, because ultimately the staircase is only as strong as its weakest step. I believe that the same is true of our performance. These highly successful people clearly do focus on their next step and ensure that they get it right! They realize that they will only reach their destination by dedicating themselves completely to each of the steps along the way. There are many people with dreams. Some might get so caught up in that dream, that they forget about the step they're taking right now. This realization represents a subtle but profound difference in the way high achievers think. It's a valuable piece of our jigsaw.

Summary

- Focus on what is right in front of you, right now.
- Fall in love with the processes, and keep your focus on them.
- Enjoy the journey, rather than focusing purely on the destination.
- Appreciate that the journey is likely to take time. There will be many twists and turns. You will probably need to 'tack'.
- It's unlikely that you'll have all the answers when you set out.
- Remember, every journey is taken one step at a time.

3
Keep It Simple

"Life is really simple, but we insist on making it complicated"
Confucius, circa 500 BC

I can see some thought bubbles appearing. 'Oh, that's easy for Confucius to say. Life probably was simple in 500 BC. What did he have to worry about? It's far more complex these days, surely. My life isn't simple. I have hundreds of things on my plate . . .'

Unfortunately, many of us do get tied up in complexity. Many people may also believe that the path to becoming better requires us to increase the complexity. However, that perception may not be entirely accurate. Mountaineer Alan Hinkes works by the KISS principle 'Keep It Stupidly Simple'. He knows that serious challenges, like getting onto an expedition and tackling a mountain, require serious focus.

This sentiment is shared by record-breaking polar explorer Ben Saunders. Ben knows that simplicity is crucial, especially when it comes to the equipment. He avoids taking anything extraneous in his pack. He will scrutinize his kit to ensure that he takes the bare minimum. But Ben does not limit this mind-set to his equipment. He applies the same thought process to his time.

"I need to be able to focus. I am planning an expedition to the South Pole now. It could get complicated because there are so many facets; permits, licenses, aviation fuel for aeroplanes, etc. I need to think, 'how much can I delegate . . . how can I simplify?'"

Ben Saunders, record-breaking polar explorer

Adventure racer Bruce Duncan also appreciates that success comes when he simplifies, rather than complicates the task, by taking out as many external distractions as possible. Bruce explained that they have to know which details to focus on when navigating. Often those details are very simple things, like finding a hand-rail to follow. Experience tells Bruce that concentrating is extremely tiring; therefore it is imperative that they keep their job as simple as possible.

"Often it's all you can do to put one foot in front of the other and follow the person in front of you. If you over-complicate things, the challenge just gets harder."

Bruce Duncan, Team GB captain
and world-leading adventure racer

Sometimes Less is More

Our own experience tells us that concentrating is tiring. When we get tired, we lose our focus more easily and start making mistakes. So it stands to reason, that if we keep things simple and reduce the number of things we're trying to concentrate on, we will be more successful. In sport, over-thinking and over-analysis can have a very negative impact on performance. Sport psychology researchers, Kristin Flegal and Michael Anderson (2008), found that when golfers try to think about more things, the performance decreases. But, it is not just true in sport. There is a new wave of neurological research, such as that conducted by Professor Daniel Weissman, which suggests that we can only think about one thing at a time (Weissman, Roberts, Visscher and Woldorff, 2006). If we are trying to focus on too many things, we inevitably end up neglecting some of those very crucial elements that we should be attending to.

> *"You obviously need to think about your game plan but I definitely try not to over-think things. I feel that if I do that, I won't play as well. You're not as relaxed if you're too busy thinking. Keeping it simple is important."*
> **Alison Waters, England international squash player**

Interestingly, England Squash's Head of Performance Keir Worth also makes a very valuable observation that we can all learn from. He explains that conditioned games are often used within squash coaching. These conditioned games restrict one of the players. Ironically, often the player that is restricted will beat the unrestricted player. Keir has noticed that the restrictions actually give players more focus because they simplify the options. If a player can only use three shots, they will make sure they use them really well.

The Power of Simplicity

If we accept that we only have a very limited capacity for focus, the big question is, *'What* should you focus on?' Answering that question becomes a lot easier when we understand our job in the simplest possible terms, and we know how to do that job well. When we have a simple, clear job, we have a very good chance of doing that job well. Obviously, we also need to have the knowledge, skills, resources and desire to do it. But, having a simple, clear task initially gives us a massive advantage. There is growing research evidence to support these ideas. For example, Stuart Bray and Lawrence Brawley (2002) identified that both task clarity and role clarity have a significant impact on performance.

When we understand the job, we're able to do it well. When we do the job well, we normally get a sense of satisfaction and fulfilment. Typically, as human beings, we like exhibiting mastery and we like to be successful in the things we do. So, when we perform well at something, we tend to want to do it again. Psychologists, such as Albert Bandura (1997), have also identified strong links between mastery, confidence, achievement and motivation. These relationships set up a positive spiral of performance.

If you're *focused* on a simple, clear job you give yourself the best chance of being successful. As a result of doing the job well, you become *confident* and enjoy doing it.

When you are confident and enjoy doing something, you're likely to be *motivated* to do it again.

There is also a negative spiral that performers often find themselves in. The negative spiral occurs when they don't have a simple, clear focus. If an athlete starts to over-think, it often causes a loss of focus on what they're doing. As a result, they make a mistake. When they make a mistake, it will often lead them to over-analyze. Normally, this results in more over-thinking and more mistakes. As you can imagine, after a while, performers get frustrated and become self-critical. As a result, they often lose confidence and inevitably motivation. This pattern is not limited to athletes. Research by Dana Lindsley and colleagues (1995) shows that very similar patterns can be seen in management and business settings.

Keeping things simple does not just benefit us as individuals. It is also crucial to the success of organizations. Jim Collins and Morten Hansen (2011) also found that successful companies had a very tangible, clear and specific set of principles that guide their operations. They note that organizations which outperform their competitors all have a SMaC recipe (Specific, Measurable and Consistent), which they adhere to.

Do the Basics VERY Well

> *"To be a great player, you have to do the basics well. To be a* world class *player, you need to do the basics very, very well. That is the difference between the world class and those just below world class. I believe that wholeheartedly."*
> **Keir Worth, England Squash's Head of Performance**

Twice Michelin-starred chef Kenny Atkinson found that simplifying his game made a huge difference to his career. Kenny had been striving towards his first Michelin star, without success, for several years. Then he arrived on the Isles of Scilly as the head chef at Teans. He told me that, because of the number of covers required, he decided to simplify everything. Rather than doing eight canapés, Kenny decided to do a couple really well. He deliberately focused his efforts on cooking very simple, high-quality dishes, using great ingredients and looking after the guests. As he explained, it wasn't complicated, but it was well executed.

> *"When I was awarded the star, my first thought was, 'How the hell have I got a star for that?' The assessor told me that my cooking had matured. I wasn't doing too much. I was*

letting the ingredients speak and producing high quality food
consistently. One of the keys to gaining a star is to be consist-
ent. Simplicity leads to consistency."
Kenny Atkinson, twice Michelin-starred chef
on being awarded his first Michelin star

In order to gain a Michelin star, it is not good enough to
produce very high quality occasionally. Consistently producing
very high quality is crucial! Kenny makes two incredibly valuable points. Firstly, he says that simplicity leads to great execution. Secondly, he says that simplicity leads to consistency.
Kenny knows that in order to achieve the standards that he
requires on a daily basis, he also needs to simplify the job for
his team. They require a simple, clear job and they need to know
how to execute it to a very high standard.

"Each of us has a function, each of us has a role and a respon-
sibility. We know the chain of command."
Gary Rossi, retired US Navy SEAL,
on the importance of simplicity to team
members in Special Forces Operations

Now, that statement may not seem particularly profound. I'm
sure you're thinking, 'yes, that's pretty obvious to me'. However,
I am constantly amazed how many of the people I work with,
who don't really know their own job in the simplest possible
terms. I am also amazed at how many organizations can't communicate their job in the simplest possible terms either. Gary
Rossi recognizes that some of the most successful organizations
on earth live by the mantra, 'keep it simple'. Gary points to very
successful business leaders such as Fred Smith at FedEx. As
Gary explained, FedEx has got a very simple mission; to deliver
a package overnight. Everything they do, from the airlines, to
the transportation systems, tracking systems and information

technology, all stems from that simple mission. According to Gary Rossi, Fred Smith is a fan of simplicity and often asks 'What's your one thing in business?'

Vance Trimble's (1993) autobiography of Fred Smith, and books such as *The Power of Simplicity*, by Jack Trout and Steve Rivkin (1998), support Gary's thoughts. The ideas are also very similar to those that I adopted with Commonwealth Champion Chris Cook during our working relationship as sport psychologist and athlete.

I started working with Chris when he came back from Beijing in 2001. He'd been to the World Student Games and finished fifth, which was disappointing from Chris' perspective. We worked together until just after Beijing 2008, that's around seven years. For the first three to four years or so of that relationship, I am embarrassed to say, we didn't actually know what Chris' job was. We thought we knew, but we got it wrong. We made the mistake of thinking his job was to win. As a swimmer, you might think his job was to win, but it wasn't. We thought his job was to make the British team. We thought his job was to break records, to secure sponsorships or to secure funding. However, none of those things were actually Chris' job.

Two Lengths of the Pool

Chris was a 100-metre swimmer in a 50-metre pool. Now it doesn't take much to do the maths. His job, very simply, was to swim two lengths of the pool as quickly as he possibly could. And that, for us, was a revelation. It had a massive impact on Chris' performance. Just simplifying his job, so Chris understood that he only needed to swim two lengths of the pool as quickly as he could, allowed him to focus on his job and become incredibly successful at it.

A Eureka Moment

Chris told a group of business leaders how he felt when we realized just how simple his job was.

When Simon first mentioned that actually my job was just to swim two lengths of the pool as fast as I could, I honestly felt like chinning (hitting) him. I thought, 'My job is a lot tougher than that, thank you very much'. It's so easy to let your ego step in the way. But actually, a lot of what I was doing at the time was not helping me swim two lengths of the pool quicker. I had a real challenge, a) accepting it and, b) committing to it. And I realized that I was the person who had to evolve and change.

The scary thing was, 60% of my week, six-tenths of what I was doing, was not helping me to swim two lengths of the pool quicker. 60% had to be thrown out; got rid of. Once I realized that, the next challenge was communicating it to the rest of the team. There was a massive team of people trying to help me get to the top. We had a physiotherapist, physiologist, Simon (the psychologist), my coaches, performance analysts, strength and conditioning coaches and loads more. So I had to let them know that I was focusing everything on going two lengths quicker, and get them to focus their efforts on this too.

Simplifying it doesn't always mean it's easy. There are lots of challenges and challenging questions along the way. But for me, I broke away from what an industry standard was. Before, I was just doing the same as everyone else was, but trying to do it 1% better. Then, I broke away from that, and started concentrating on what I was doing.

To make this work, Chris and I also spent time understanding exactly *how* he was going to swim two lengths of the pool as fast as he could. What was it that he needed to do? What were the most important things? What would have the most significant impact? There were hundreds of component parts to his performance. We needed to understand how they worked, and how they contributed. Once we knew this, Chris could devote his time to those things that he knew were most crucial. As a result, his training and preparation became far more effective. However, the benefit was not limited to training. Having a very simple focus also helped Chris in competition.

> *"I was so focused; I didn't even think I was in the final. I was just trying to swim two lengths of the baths (pool) as fast as I could. That's where my mentality was. It wasn't about beating other people, the medals, or the records. It was all condensed down into swimming two lengths of the pool as quick as I could."*
> **Chris Cook, double Olympian and Commonwealth champion, reflecting on his gold-medal winning performance in the Commonwealth 100-metres final of 2006**

Of course, these principles can be applied a lot more widely that just swimming, or indeed sport. I have found that whatever the domain, understanding your job and your key processes in the simplest possible terms can be incredibly powerful. In Chris' case, it was transformational. On a daily basis, Chris would assess how each and every session contributed to swimming two lengths quicker. He would scrutinize his training schedule according to whether it passed this acid test. In doing so, he became infinitely more effective!

When we are effective, we get more from every moment.

Those who get more from every moment, become much better, much quicker.

Simplicity and Effectiveness

Recently, I have been working with a Managing Director of a multinational I.T. business. For many years, he has worked toward goals which were invariably related to outcome targets such as turnover and profit targets. Like Chris Cook, there were about two hundred potential things that this Managing Director could do to help him reach his goals. Unlike Chris Cook, he had not simplified his role or worked out which of those things provided the greatest contribution. Therefore, he tried to do all two hundred. As a result, he was not particularly effective. He worked far too many hours, often missed his goals and regularly became frustrated.

It is probably no great surprise that extremely successful people understand the importance of simplicity. When Chris Cook understood that his job was simply to swim two lengths of the pool as quickly as he could, he became exceptionally effective. He used it as a benchmark, and ditched those things that didn't help him swim up and down the pool quicker. He devoted his time, energy and focus to those things that had the greatest impact on his speed over two lengths.

However, it's not just Chris Cook that applied this thought process. Ultra-distance runner Andy McMenemy used almost the same approach during 'Challenge 66'. He explained that he also simplified everything. He started by focusing on his own job and letting his team get on with theirs. Andy also told me that he had five things that he needed to do, in order to be successful. He needed to pace himself properly during each run, ensure he was hydrated, recuperate well, ensure he got the right nutrition and enough rest. That was his job.

Keir Worth employs the same mentality at an organizational level with England Squash. He realizes that there are many potential projects and a huge variety of avenues and opportunities available. However, Keir and his team understand that they need to be incredibly pragmatic. Everything needs to translate to the performance of the players on court. Keir often asks, 'What difference will it make? How much impact will it have?' In his words, 'It has to count towards making us the best in the world.'

In reality, the high achievers that I interviewed have equally complex tasks as the rest of us. However, there is a difference in the way they perceive their tasks. They perceive them as simple because they are very clear about what they need to do in order to be successful. They are focused on their processes, and executing those processes to the best of their ability. Unlike many of us, they do not seem to bring emotional baggage into their tasks. They don't appear to get tied down by the 'pressure' of expectation, the need to impress someone else, or the need to hit targets to achieve a sense of self-worth. In many cases I suspect that 'complexity' is often mistaken for 'lack of clarity'.

There is a strong message here. Simplicity is integral to becoming the best you can be. Clarity of focus also helps us to get the basics right. As Keir Worth pointed out, getting the basics right is absolutely central to great performances. It also helps us to produce our best performances consistently. Kenny Atkinson found that when he achieved consistent high performance, his first Michelin star followed. Of course, consistent high performance is not only critical if you are seeking a Michelin star.

It also separates the world's best from the rest in sport, business and any other domain you care to think of. Consistent high performance requires us to be focused on those simple processes! Having a tight focus helps us to ensure we maintain quality in those things that are really important. You don't need to be a genius to recognize that maintaining exceptionally high quality is key if you really want to shine.

Summary

- Often, less is more.
- A tight focus will help you become more effective in every moment.
- Focus on your key processes and on doing the basics extremely well.
- Simplicity and clarity will help you to achieve consistent high performance.
- Do you know your 'Two Lengths of the Pool'?

4
Don't Compromise

In reality, the *no compromise* approach has to live within a context. There have to be compromises somewhere. As we will see through the course of this chapter, even world-class people and world-class organizations do make compromises. Rather than asking whether they make compromises or not, perhaps it is better to ask *when* and *where* they make compromises. What things will they compromise on and what will they absolutely not compromise on? The answers to these questions help us to really start understanding how very successful people think and how they make their decisions on a daily basis. This understanding allows us to really get under the skin of the issues, and to see what makes them very different from the rest.

Team GB captain Bruce Duncan understands that there are some things he has to compromise on and some things that he will not. For example, he's happy to compromise on comfort. He will often be uncomfortable for five or six days, because the goal is worth it. Bruce also knows that he has to make choices about the amount of kit he can take, which ultimately means he needs to compromise. However, there are certain things that he cannot afford to compromise on, such as nutrition. Running out of energy can be costly. As he explained, fatigue leads to mistakes. Making mistakes often leads to self-doubt, which can result in a massive negative spiral.

"There are some things where the consequences of getting it wrong are dire. I never compromise on safety. I know that there is an inherent risk in what I do, which means that everything has to be very measured . . . recently there was a weather window to get us onto the Arctic Ocean but we couldn't identify a clear window to get out, so we called it off. I always have to weigh up my skills and knowledge against the risks."

Ben Saunders, record-breaking polar explorer

It is a sentiment that is echoed by Michelin-starred chef Kenny Atkinson. He explains that when a chef makes a mistake with expensive ingredients, there is a temptation to serve the dish rather than bin it. Kenny realizes in the long run, that approach will cost a chef a lot more than the ingredients.

It All Comes Down to Choice

The decision to compromise or not, comes down to choice. Some might choose to compromise quality in order to maximize profit. Others make choices that have a higher financial cost, but safeguard quality. These decisions are the real-life, everyday choices that all of us make.

As a professional squash player Alison Waters is self-employed and makes these sorts of decisions on a daily basis. For Alison, preparation takes priority and she sacrifices a lot in order to get the best preparation she can. For example, she will not compromise the quality of preparation based on the financial cost. Alison understands that the life-span of a professional squash player is pretty short and that she has to make the most of each moment she has.

Double Olympian Chris Cook has also made decisions about whether to focus on financial gain or performance gain. At one point, Chris was offered a sponsorship deal by Adidas. It was worth a huge amount to Chris; enough to pay off the mortgage on his house. However, he knew that the Adidas swimsuit actually made him a tenth of a second slower in the pool. Chris had already committed everything to swimming two lengths of the pool as quickly as he could. Therefore, he turned down the deal.

> *"It looked like a tough decision. Loads of people asked me what the heck I was doing. They told me to get my head read. But for me it was really simple. It was not going to help me swim two lengths as quick as I could so I had to get rid of it."*
> **Chris Cook, double Olympian and Commonwealth finalist, on turning down a lucrative sponsorship deal**

The Core Purpose

It seems that their decisions were made according to one powerful driver. World-class performers understand their focus. They know their core purpose. In many cases, their primary aim is not to increase their bank balance. Their aim is to excel in their field. Chris Cook's job was not to make as much money as he could from swimming; it was to swim two lengths of a pool as quickly as he could. Chris was willing to sacrifice a six-figure sponsorship deal to do that. You might think that this mentality is fine for an athlete, but does not apply to business. However, even when they are in business, the highly successful people I interviewed, often prioritized quality over profit. At the first Be World-Class Conference, World Barista Champion James Hoffmann explained that quality, not size or profit, was the key driver in his coffee roasting business.

Ultra-distance runner Andy McMenemy emphasizes how his decisions regarding when to compromise were also driven by an understanding of his core purpose. He knew the importance of delivering on his five key processes. Therefore, he decided to sacrifice some of the speaking engagement and public relations exercises, to protect these critical processes.

A Strength of Purpose

Mountaineer Alan Hinkes takes this mentality even further. I asked Alan if he thought that his decision making, and willingness to compromise, changes as he gets closer to his goal. Did he get tempted to compromise safety, or push too hard as he neared the summit of his 13th or 14th 8000-metre peak?

They say the brain doesn't work quite as well with the lack of oxygen, but I always thought mine did. I have stopped a few times and slapped myself around mentally. Stop and assess this slope; what do you think is the percentage chance that it will avalanche? What percentage chance are you happy to accept?

I certainly did this on my 13th mountain, Dhaulagiri. About an hour or so from the summit, there was a point where I thought about whether to turn back – off the top of my head, I figured there was a 50% chance of avalanche. But then I thought, 'If I come back another time, I'll have to go through massive danger just to get back to where I am right now, within an hour of the summit. And this is my 13th I've only got two left.'

I re-assessed the situation and stopped for a while, with about 100 metres to go. I dug a little pit in the snow to investigate the layers of snow. This took about half an hour, which people would not normally do. They would either crack on or back off. I saw that there were layers of snow and that it could avalanche, but probably not 50% chance, though you can never tell exactly.

If I was anywhere else I'd have backed off or tried a different slope, but this was one of my 8000'ers. So I thought, 'No, it's probably about 10% and I said to my mate, 'Come on, let's risk it.'

Now, a 10% risk is pretty high! You wouldn't jump on a train at Darlington to go to King's Cross if they said there was a 10% chance you were going to get killed.

When I had made the conscious decision to do all the 8000-metre peaks, there were things that I did not compromise on; that's why I accepted such a high risk-level. If I had got it wrong, my daughter would have been left without a Dad. I knew that would be very selfish and I'm aware that there is a certain amount of selfishness there. Once I'd decided to do them all, there was no compromise with my life. That sounds a bit strange, but it's true, there was no compromise with my life. I wouldn't say that I was prepared to die, but I obviously was prepared to die because I had to do all 14. I wasn't gung-ho. I have always been a realist. I suppose I am very lucky to be alive. Most people who try to do what I've done don't survive.

"

Alan's account shows that the strength of purpose was so great, that he made some incredible decisions. Ultimately he chose to accept a 10% risk of being killed, rather than compromise on completing the 14 peaks. Climbing ever higher and taking on the challenges of the mountains, was Alan's purpose. He didn't compromise this for money, or even the risk of losing his life.

There are Always Some Compromises

In reality, compromises do have to be made in life. Keir Worth's job might be to help keep England Squash at the top of the world, but he is not blessed with unlimited resources and so compromises do have to be made. Keir explains that decisions are often driven by an understanding of their core purpose; producing the best squash players and teams in the world. Often his team have to make difficult decisions, such as recognizing a need to cut players, or choosing where to allocate their limited resources. They simply have not got the money to do what they'd like to do. Keir knows that they can always be more effective and make better use of their budget, which inevitably means making difficult decisions. In order to make those tough decisions, the team need to be able to challenge each other.

> *"You have to have discussions, arguments and even fights about the decisions we need to make and we have to exhaust every option. It is tough."*
> **Keir Worth, England Squash's Head of Performance**

Keir has developed a High Performance Unit, which operates with openness, honesty and trust. This allows them to be critical of each other, challenge each other, and be able to give and take clean feedback. It means that they can take things on the chin and not just dismiss them. The result is that decisions are made under an extreme level of scrutiny, which protects the quality.

Don't Compromise Quality

In addition to scrutinizing the way in which they allocate resources, the England Squash team work hard to ensure that they attend to the tiny details. They know that everything they do should be done properly. This mentality starts with the High Performance Unit, but extends to the coaches and ultimately the players. As an organization, they foster good habits. The 'little things', such as maintaining training diaries, are considered important at England Squash. In addition, Keir and his team have worked hard to ensure that all the coaches deliver consistent messages, have common expectations and therefore create a solid culture. These things don't happen by accident. They require a great deal of thought. It is the result of deliberate design and constant review by Keir and his team. Ensuring that the ethos of the High Performance Unit is translated throughout the sport is not an easy task, but it is one that Keir believes will make a difference.

Keir's account clearly shows that England Squash don't compromise on their core purpose, their standards or their quality. Attention to detail it seems, goes hand in hand with the refusal to compromise on standards. In fact, author Keith Black (2010) illustrates that other organizations who have reached the pinnacle of their field, such as Walt Disney World Resorts, also have this partnership between standards and attention to detail at their foundation.

Tiny Things Make a Big Difference

Many elite athletes know that the margin between success and failure is often minute. Therefore, those at the very top work extremely hard to make tiny gains.

"The 1% changes might make the difference now, and that 1% is more difficult to get than when I started out. The 1%'s are easy to get when you first start out but now the gap is so small that the little things are those that make the biggest differences."
Alison Waters, England International squash player

Bruce Duncan shares a similar view on the importance of attending to detail and preparation in adventure racing. His preparation for the Wenger Patagonian Expedition race starts five months before the event. Bruce knows that equipment failure can be catastrophic. There are no bike shops in the wilderness of the Chilean Andes, so although he can take a basic repair kit, he cannot cater for every eventuality. Therefore, Bruce ensures that his equipment is fully serviced and renewed before the team departs. Specialist kit needs to be ordered well in advance. He even packs his kit weeks in advance to allow him the chance to check and re-check every element.

The cost of not getting things absolutely right can be considerable. Ben Saunders lost an expedition and a year's worth of work in 2008, when a ski binding broke. It was a £150k expedition which failed, because of a piece of kit that cost less than ten pence. In 2010, Ben had to abort a Polar expedition because a fuel container leaked and contaminated his food. The seal that failed was worth about one penny. Ben explained that although the seal was tight when they ran the checks indoors, it didn't mean it would be tight at -40°C. Having learned the hard way, Ben now views his equipment as a chain and looks to identify the weak links.

It is a lesson that we can all learn from. Often success and failure are separated by the smallest of margins. One or two minor details can prove to be costly. If we let the 'little things' slip, there is a chance that they will become 'big things'. Some details can seem almost insignificant, but they can have a knock on effect. Little things can accumulate, compound and become big things.

As these accounts show, consistently attending to details is crucial to success. Ultra-distance athlete Andy McMenemy realized that he needed to pace his runs well in order to avoid burning out. If Andy ran at his natural pace, he would burn out and inevitably pay for it the following day. Therefore, he had to deliberately slow his pace, which is not easy to do. It required a great deal of focus to avoid slipping into his natural pace. Although Andy had a simple focus, he needed a great deal of discipline to stay on course. In addition, Andy made sure he drank 300–500 ml of water every hour and ate 6000 calories a day, which he found very difficult. He also had a regime of hot and cold bathing, massage and rehabilitation. Although it was very tough and very regimented, Andy knew how crucial each element was.

"Certain things can't be compromised if you want to be successful."
Andy McMenemy, record-breaking ultra-distance runner

Consistently applying simple processes often requires a great deal of discipline and focus. Although slowing down sounds easier, it is something that Andy had to consciously think about. When we're tired or we have a lot on our plate, sometimes details slip. The accounts of these highly successful people illustrate that the tiny details need to be protected.

Attending to the Details Requires Effort!

Attending to the tiny details requires a great deal of effort, but ignoring them can be costly. Mountaineer Alan Hinkes always makes sure that his tent is spotless. Although it may seem unnecessary to some people, cleanliness, hygiene and waste disposal are important issues on a mountain. If Alan throws a used tea bag out of his tent it could burst, scattering tea leaves across the snow. If he then collects a bag full of dirty snow to melt for drinking water, he stands a greater chance of developing diarrhoea.

It can be easy to ignore tiny details like this. Alan also makes sure that he spends 15–20 minutes in the morning warming his toes, socks and boots, in order to prevent frost bite. Many mountaineers don't bother, especially if they're behind time and are worried about setting out late. If they are pushed for time, they may only do part of the job. For example, they might warm their feet and socks, but not the boots. As a result, they put warm feet and socks into cold boots and end up with cold feet anyway. Those people then normally face a tough choice when their feet start to freeze; either crack on and get frost bite, or turn around. In the 30 years that Alan has been climbing, he has never suffered from frost bite.

Alan and I went on to discuss the consequences that follow, if you do not attend to those details on a mountain. It stands to reason that those who are cold and wet are unlikely to be completely focused on the task in hand. Half the brain will be tied up thinking, 'I've got a bad belly' or 'my feet hurt', and consequently, they won't focus. Even in daily tasks, if we're cold, wet, tired or hungry, we don't do them well. Alan explained that if you're on a mountain and you don't do your tasks well, you're in trouble; you don't make good decisions and you become clumsy. Alan remembers seeing other mountaineers who became tired, demoralized and who consequently lost their discipline. This is a great illustration that letting the 'little things' slip can ultimately cause catastrophic problems, when those tiny details accumulate and compound.

> *"On the mountain, you have to discipline yourself to do those little things and pay attention to those small things. It may sound obvious, but eating regularly and drinking regularly is crucial but some don't. Attention to details often makes the difference between life and death. Little things build up."*
> **Alan Hinkes, world-leading mountaineer**

Like Alan Hinkes, former US Navy SEAL Gary Rossi also appreciates that the tiny details could mean the difference between life and death. Gary told me that several days before embarking on a mission, the SEAL team would go through a thorough briefing. This strategic plan covered every element in excruciating detail. They would analyze the terrain, identify the 'friendlies' and enemies, insertion, extraction, weapons, contingency plans and so on. As Gary explained, nothing was left to chance. Each person knew their role within the chain of command and knew exactly what they needed to do.

> *"If you don't get the tiny details absolutely right, the smallest thing can cause an absolute catastrophe."*
> **Gary Rossi, retired US Navy SEAL**

Details and Confidence

It's clear to see that world-class people know the importance of detail and preparation. They understand which details are really important, the mission critical details, and they absolutely do not compromise on those. It is integral to their preparation and gives them the confidence to embark on some incredibly demanding challenges. Interestingly, feeling prepared often underpins our confidence. This relationship is one that can be seen across multiple domains. Katie Wiggins-Dohlvik and her colleagues (2009) studied the performance of surgeons during critical situations. They concluded that practice and preparation underpinned the levels of competence and confidence, which enabled high levels of performance in critical situations.

Have I Done Everything Possible?

Olympic swimmer Chris Cook understands the importance of turning over every stone.

Going into any race, if I felt nervous, there was probably a part of me that wasn't quite prepared. If I had that nervous feeling that makes you feel sick, it was because I had maybe dipped out of a part of training, hadn't quite turned over every single stone, and that was another aspect that we started to work on.

Attention to detail is something we just couldn't afford to let go of. Turning up to championships and nailing the race was the goal. But you can't plan for every eventuality.

That's what preparation gives you. It's about being at your best when it counts. That comes from working every day and putting those tiny little building blocks in. And I'm going to say this now; it feels like you're getting nowhere. You can see everyone around you doing their thing, and it feels like you're getting nowhere. But eventually, all those little building blocks add up and get their opportunity to shine.

Understanding the Critical Details

Clearly, attention to detail and preparation helps high achievers to execute their performance to a high standard. However, attention to detail can have more than one dimension. There are dimensions that go beyond execution of the task.

James Hoffmann explains the multiple levels of attention to detail that are required to become World Barista Champion. It would seem obvious to many people that producing a world-class cup of coffee is a pre-requisite for anyone wishing to become a World Barista Champion. There are many technical elements that require extreme attention to detail such as the coarseness of the grind, the need for the ground coffee to be evenly packed inside the handle and the brewing time, which all competitors are judged on. However, James also recognizes that anybody at world level is likely to achieve 95–98% of the available points. He realizes that competitive advantage must be gained elsewhere. It is not enough to simply make great coffee. The aim must be to *serve* great coffee:

> *"Where the game is now won and lost, is in the way you make the sensory judges feel. Taste is largely objective. Enjoyment is highly subjective. They will all taste the same thing, but their enjoyment of it is highly malleable. How much do I enjoy you making me coffee? I think this is what it boils down to."*
> **James Hoffmann, World Barista Champion**

This realization is relevant to the vast majority of businesses. James knows that creating a fantastic experience is paramount to his success as a competitive barista and crucial to the success of his business. Therefore, James spends a great deal of time, effort and thought to ensuring that customers experience enjoyment. He goes out of his way to push his team to bring customer experience to the forefront.

> ## The Details that Really Matter
>
> James Hoffmann created an environment that really tested his team's ability to deliver the fine details:
>
> *We ran a pop-up café for three months. It was brewed coffee only. It was just black coffee, no milk, no sugar, no espresso. It was not cheap. No take-away. The offer was simple – come and have coffee with us. It could have been a very dry and unpleasant experience. So we spent a huge amount of time and effort on service and service training, every day. We found that normally, a barista's tips in the UK are negligible; they wouldn't buy you anything. It's really non-existent. However, we had one barista that would regularly take home £30– £40 in tips. And bear in mind, we'd make a quarter of the number of drinks of a regular café. What was going on? British people are notorious for not tipping. There are businesses in this world that liberate vast amounts of money from my pocket and I am very happy for them to have it. I enjoy the product and the experience of buying that product from them. There are some businesses that you love being customer of.*
>
> **James Hoffmann, World Barista Champion**

And that's not just true in the coffee business. As you might expect, this phenomenon is well documented in hospitality (Michelli, 2008), and retail (Smith and Wheeler, 2002). Crucially, understanding the importance of the customer experience also helps James decide where he will, and will not, make compromises in his roastery business. Although James is aware of the demand for pre-ground coffee, he does not sell it, even though he knows that there is a market and a strong commercial argument. However, James knows that the retail price of a bag of beans will be the same, whether they are whole roasted beans, or pre-ground. The problem is, he also knows that the experience will be very different. Those that buy a bag of beans and grind them at home will have a phenomenal experience. The person who buys the pre-ground will have an okay experience for exactly the same price. James does not want to sell bad value for money. He would rather lose the sale than compromise the experience.

Decisions such as these separate James from his peers. How many other businesses make the decision to lose a sale, rather than compromise on customer experience? These choices differentiate exceptional people. Those at the very pinnacle of their field often understand how crucial it is to protect things that may seem trivial to others.

A great deal of time, effort and thought is required to ensure great customer experience. Chef Kenny Atkinson ensures that the volume of the live piano in the dining room is matched to the height of the room. This allows customers to hear it, without the piano over-dominating the room. It seems that he sees the volume of the piano in the same way as balancing flavours in a dish. Kenny also ensures that the wines are matched to the individual courses, so that the flavours between food and wine are always well-balanced. Even the selection of dining chairs requires careful thought.

"Believe it or not, we've been looking at new chairs for the dining room. It's been a long process finding the ones that are just right. Little touches like that make a difference."
Kenny Atkinson, twice Michelin-starred chef

Kenny Atkinson and James Hoffmann clearly understand that the tiniest of details actually make all the difference. Those things that they work on tirelessly to protect are the things that differentiate them and make them world-class in their fields.

Being Aware of the Details

So, why is it that world-class operators have this incredible attention to detail? Perhaps the answer lies in their ability to always look for ways to improve. They constantly seek the next level. They see that they are not quite there yet, they haven't reached perfection and there is more to get.

High achievers see those things because they look for them!

Their *never satisfied* mentality drives them to challenge themselves ever harder. As they do so, they become aware of the subtleties that make a difference at the highest level. They understand what they must do to separate themselves from their competition.

James Hoffmann looked for ways to make tiny changes in presentation, which would create significantly different experiences for barista judges. He experimented with different ways to describe flavours. In doing so, he found that subtle changes in his description resulted in a very different experience for the judges. James deliberately uses phrases that tap into the senses and he draws on familiar experiences. He understands the importance of evoking emotion as well as imparting information.

"

Subtle Changes Make Huge Differences

James Hoffmann describes how very subtle changes helped make him a World Champion.

If I said to you that the espresso will smell of black-currants and toast, that sounds okay. But if I say that this espresso is like hot, buttered toast, smoth-ered in blackcurrant jam, that is a very different description that pushes a different button. You're likely to think, 'I know that smell and I like it . . . I know what you mean, that's lovely', and your saliva goes and you think, 'that's going to be nice.'

I could say it smells like chocolate, or I could say it smells like a tray of brownies fresh from the oven. They both smell of chocolate, but which one do I want to try?

"

It Does not Happen by Accident

I believe that this level of awareness doesn't develop by chance. Equally, I don't believe that it is a product of innate talent. As we dedicate ourselves to excelling in our field, we begin to notice the tiny details and we focus on getting them right. Anyone who has an insatiable curiosity and a desire to become the best they can be is more likely to see these opportunities. Curiosity keeps us searching for more. But, where does this insatiable curiosity come from? Perhaps it is born out of passion, or an intrinsic love for what we do. Psychologist George Lowenstein (1994) suggests that curiosity can be viewed as a passion, with all the motivational intensity implied by the term. He also describes it as a passion for learning, an intrinsically motivated desire to understand and to master our environment.

These accounts present a couple of strong and clear messages. High achievers do things that other people simply don't do. They chase down the tiny details. In many cases, they seem to go out of their way to understand the critical details that will set them apart. It is also clear that these people are happy to invest significant time, energy and resources to ensure they nail these details.

There is a clear pattern. They do not compromise on standards or quality. They do not compromise on their core purpose. In order to do this, they often compromise on their own comfort instead. In some cases it may be physical comfort or mental comfort (i.e. relaxation). In other cases, it may be financial; they choose to compromise income or profit over quality.

It seems that world-class people are implicitly aware that if they do the things most people do, they will get the results that everyone else gets. Following that path would lead them to become ordinary, rather than extraordinary.

> *"You have got to be able to do the little things, and make the effort to do them . . . yes, it's harder to do, but it's more important because it's the little things that will cost you."*
> **Alan Hinkes, world-leading mountaineer**

Summary

- Compromises are driven by choice.
- Never compromise on 'the core' or 'quality'.

- In order to protect the quality, we often need to make tough decisions.
- Take time to understand the crucial details that will set you apart.
- Make the effort to get the tiny things right – ultimately it's those tiny things that will make a big difference.

5
Push The Envelope

The world-class people and organizations that I studied are different from the rest. By definition, they have achieved a great deal more than the vast majority of their peers. Their achievements are extraordinary. In some cases, the feats are incredible. As we have already discovered, if we want to achieve the extraordinary, we cannot do ordinary things. Extraordinary feats require us to explore new territory, break down boundaries and barriers; push the envelope.

The Centre for Life in the UK is a great example. As an organization, they have broken the mould. They have created something truly unique and world-leading in the field of science and medicine. The centre is self-funding and self-sustaining, which in itself is very unusual; however, its uniqueness stems from its operating model, which brings together many disciplines from medical science in one place. This cross-discipline model is ground-breaking and has smashed down a lot of long-standing barriers. The Centre for Life brings together research units, an Ethics Institute, several practicing clinics, commercial incubation units, as well as the public engagement and education centre. As Linda explains, all of this has enabled the Centre to create a unique environment that allows pioneering research to thrive:

"There is always pressure from government to reduce the timeframes from laboratory to bedside. I think that it helps having a diverse range of people, from the laboratory, clinical practice and the world of commerce, in close physical proximity. That can help us to become more effective."
Linda Conlon, Centre for Life Chief Executive

As a result, the Centre for Life has been able to make some pioneering discoveries. The Stem Cell Institute at the Centre for Life actually cloned the first human embryo! Although we will each have our own moral and ethical perspective on pioneering science, it is hard to deny the ground-breaking and world-leading nature of it.

Within this book, I am not proposing to make any moral or ethical judgement on cloning the human embryo or any other area of research. However, I do recognize that it represents a significant advancement in science and is a world-leading move, just as world records are in sports. It is obvious from Linda's account, that the Centre for Life is exploring new territory and pushing the boundaries of science and medicine. The question is: how are they doing it? How are they thinking?

Big changes provide big challenges. Often, there is a huge amount of resistance. For Linda at the Centre for Life, this might come in the form of inertia, or maybe even opposition. In establishing the Centre for Life, Linda faced a multitude of opposition, apathy and competition – all of which she had to overcome just to get the project approved. They also needed to persuade the stakeholders from the various research institutes, clinics, commercial and educational centres to come together and invest in a brand-new, untried and untested model.

"We had to THINK BIG! We needed to have an exciting vision and have absolute belief in it. To make it happen, it really is 99% perspiration and 1% inspiration. You have to have an incredible amount of tenacity. We needed a huge amount of energy to overcome the inertia and the apathy. We needed energy and passion. Passion is more important than skill if you want to make things happen."

Linda Conlon, Centre for Life Chief Executive,
on describing how they overcame
the challenges of establishing the Centre

The story of the Centre for Life shows some of the challenges that stop many people from pushing their envelope. It requires a great deal of energy and tenacity. The journey tends to be tough and incredibly challenging. Very rarely do things work well at the first time of asking. Inevitably, pushing the boundaries requires us to try and fail.

Into the Unknown!

When we push the boundaries, we enter virgin territory. We take on challenges we've not experienced before. Our own life experience will tell us that there can be a multitude of demands that we've not encountered before. As we push ourselves and leave our familiar territory, the challenges can become uncomfortable and demand more of us. Polar explorer Ben Saunders knows that world record-breaking attempts inevitably require him and his team, to take on an array of challenges that they have never encountered. He understands that he begins to push the limits when he conceives the challenge. This is when he sets the bar. In 2012, Ben will attempt a four-month, 1800-mile expedition from the coast of Antarctica to the South

Pole and back, on foot! It is the first time anyone will have completed the trek unsupported. As he explained, when he sets the bar that high, every other challenge scales up. He requires more funding, there are more potential complications, he needs more training, there are more logistical considerations, and so on. Over a coffee, Ben outlined a training event that he was about to embark on in Scotland. He was taking his team into the wilderness on the Isle of Skye so that he could test the human dynamic and the relationships. Ben knows that this element will be tested more than ever in Antarctica.

Ben Saunders illustrates a very important point. High achievers often do set the bar much higher than their peers. In doing so, they raise the level of challenge. This forces them to push their own boundaries and do things that they've never done before. Typically, this process also leads to mistakes, failure and therefore an awful lot of learning. As a result, they develop new knowledge and acquire new skills. Put simply, they become better.

Prepare to Fail

Inevitably, pushing the boundaries means experiencing failure. Kenny Atkinson has been awarded two Michelin stars and is working on a third. Many people would imagine that he is now past the point where he fails or makes mistakes. However, the reality is significantly different. When creating new dishes, Kenny will often make ten or more attempts. He explained that it is rare that he'll get it right first time. Sometimes he will end up scrapping his dish completely and starting again. In order to create his winning dish for the *Great British Menu* competition, Kenny went through dozens of stages and different combinations. Often his chefs would tell him the dish was great, but Kenny persisted because he knew it wasn't quite right. At each stage he would try different ingredients, flavours and textures until he was happy.

I believe it is a popular misconception that world-class people make few mistakes and that they tend to get things right first time. As Kenny illustrates, he is not worried about getting it right first time, or getting the approval of his fellow chefs. He's not interested in creating the dish quickly. He's focused on getting his dishes to be the best they can be. This mind-set is also obvious in others who have reached the pinnacle of their field.

Olympic swimmer Chris Cook spent years trying to perfect elements of his race. Chris came back from his first ever international appearance very disappointed; he finished eighth. In his eyes, he had failed. So Chris, his coach and I, watched the video of the race to see where it had gone wrong. It didn't take us long. Chris' start was, in his words, 'pretty terrible'. Over the first 15 metres of the race, Chris had lost two or three metres to his competition. From the very start, he was forced to play catch-up. That was the spark that drove Chris, myself and the rest of the team for the next few years. The team consisted of physiologists, bio-mechanists, performance analysts and various coaches. We worked for hundreds of hours to shave a few tenths of a second off his start time. We also applied the same mentality to his first length, his turn, the return length and his finish, in order to nail down the tiny details. This all came about because of a failure.

"Every time I was confronted by a failure, or I didn't quite hit that target, I just viewed it as a bunch of opportunities. It was a chance to take another step forwards. It wasn't quite good enough but I could find out how to get it good enough."
**Chris Cook, double Olympian and
Commonwealth champion**

Failure – the Catalyst for Success

Interestingly, Chris gives an insight into a key trait that many proven winners seem to have. They seem to have a different view of failure and mistakes to other people. Chris views failure as a 'bunch of opportunities'. He's not alone. Sport psychologist Susan Halden-Brown (2003) advocates embracing mistakes to improve sports performance. She also recognizes that 'failure' and 'mistakes' are incredibly valuable for anyone who strives to excel. These sentiments are not limited to the world of sport. Arguably, mistakes and failures are potentially valuable for all of us.

> *"I don't like it if I can't get something right. If I can't do something, it makes me more determined to get it right . . . I guess I don't like to finish on a bad exercise or a bad set, or something. I just have to get it right."*
>
> **Alison Waters,**
> **England International squash player**

Many of the highly successful people that I interviewed share a similar perspective. They seem to view their knowledge and skills as a work in progress. Chris Cook also worked for years on elements of his performance. He constantly reviewed his performance to identify areas that he could refine. He knew that however good he was, there was always room for improvement. As he became more proficient, the potential for further improvement became less obvious. Once he'd got the 'big things' right, he began to notice the subtle improvements that needed to be made.

> *"I remember feeling that my big toe was sticking out and feeling the drag coming off of it when we were working on*

starts. It sounds like a small thing, but it meant it wasn't quite right. I think I was always searching for that perfect start."

**Chris Cook, double Olympian
and Commonwealth champion**

Mistakes Provide Focus and Motivation

Alison and Chris show how they use their mistakes and imperfections as a reference point. The 'mistakes' highlight elements of the performance that they need to focus on. It gives them a clear focus for their training and helps them hone their practices. In essence, the mistakes help Chris and Alison understand how to improve their performances. Having worked with both of them, I also know that they actively look for the imperfections in their game. It is a key part of their relentless mission to constantly improve and become the best that they can be. By identifying and working on these imperfections, they know that they are becoming a better athlete. As a result, the 'mistakes' become a positive motivational force.

"I see mistakes as a positive. The mistakes help you work out what you need to be doing, so you can work on those little things. You have to make mistakes to become stronger in a way. If you didn't make mistakes, you wouldn't really learn would you?"

Alison Waters, England International squash player

Helping us to focus our practice, training and development is obviously a very valuable element. However, Alison identifies another very important facet. Mistakes help her to know when she's operating outside of her comfort zone. If she's not making mistakes, she's probably not pushing the boundaries. If she's not pushing the boundaries, she's not improving.

The high achievers that I interviewed appear to share a common view of mistakes and imperfections. They do not try to forget about them. They are not aiming to get over them. In fact, their approach seems to be the reverse. These world-class performers look for, and actively *use* their mistakes.

> *"If I know how I'm going to do it, the challenge is not hard enough."*
> **Ben Saunders, record-breaking polar explorer**

Adventure racer Bruce Duncan also recognizes the power of making mistakes. As he explains, his 'monumental cock-ups' have helped to remind him of the things he was doing right. Bruce now habitually keeps his compass with him whilst navigating, after getting lost for an hour and a half during a selection race for the Great Britain orienteering team. As Bruce knows, maps can be wrong but the compass keeps pointing north. That experience now gives Bruce the conviction in what he's doing, which is vital.

> *"Until you make a mistake, you don't know what you're doing right."*
> **Bruce Duncan, Team GB captain**
> **and world-leading adventure racer**

It is not unusual for our greatest lessons to come in those times of greatest failure. The disasters often hold the most powerful lessons. World Barista Champion James Hoffmann has also experienced this first hand. In 2005 he made a colossal mistake in the finals of the UK championship. He ended up running so far over time that he was disqualified. Had he finished in time, James would have comfortably won the competition. James explained that at the time, he was devastated, but the experience was incredibly valuable. He now understands that mistakes actually give him a great deal of confidence. James knows that once he fixes the mistake, his performance will be much better.

Mistakes Provide Confidence

I have seen very successful athletes using their mistakes to increase their confidence (that's right, *increase* their confidence). Imagine two athletes, who both have disappointing performances. The first athlete feels upset and gets disheartened, so they try to forget the performance. They go back into training and do the same things they did before. The second athlete also feels upset, but decides to go through the uncomfortable task of reviewing the performance in detail. They identify the things that went wrong and work hard on them in training. A couple of weeks later, they can see tangible improvements in those areas of their game. The second athlete is not making the same mistakes now. Who do you think will go into their next competition feeling more confident?

Ben Saunders remembers his first polar expedition. In his words, it was a 'complete failure'. He did not make it to the Pole, he got frostbite, suffered from hunger and got attacked by a polar bear. The experience left Ben feeling devastated, exhausted and financially he was left with next to nothing. That would probably be enough to stop most people from going back to the Arctic. However, as Ben reviewed the expedition, he realized that he'd taken a pretty radical approach on his first attempt. He concluded that he probably hadn't trained hard enough for the physical challenge; he was inexperienced and under-prepared. In hindsight, Ben became aware that there was not one big thing that caused him to fail, but a combination of many little things. He made changes to his preparation, equipment and nutrition because he could see how they could all be improved. Armed with this experience, Ben's next expedition was far more successful.

"

Sometimes Powerful Lessons Hurt

Double Olympian Chris Cook also understands how learning from failure can be the driver for success. Here is another excerpt from our presentation to business leaders in the UK, where Chris describes his experience of his first Olympic Games in Athens, 2004:

I'd reached the Olympic Games. I can't tell you how chuffed I was. We had been working really hard on my race plan. My plan was built on taking the first half of the race at a steady pace and finishing strong. And so I went out to Athens with my race plan.

When you get to an Olympic event, before the race, you get called into a marshal room. It's a tiny room and it's full of competitors who want to strip you of your dreams. They want that Olympic gold, and you want it. Just as I am walking through that door, my boss, Bill, a big Aussie [Australian] guy and a revered character, came over and grabbed me to one side. He said, 'I don't know what your race plan is sunshine, but I want you to go out as quick as you can and hold on in this race.'

'Yes Bill, yes Bill, I'll do that, no problem Bill'.'
So I went out and did that. But it became one of the biggest regrets of my career. I raced somebody else's race. I didn't even make it through the semi-final.

When I came back from Athens, we did a lot of thinking and talking. Why had I let that affect me? Why had I let somebody influence my swimming?

> *A year later, it was the World Championships in Montreal and pretty much everyone (the best swimmers in the world) was there. And it was almost a carbon copy. I walked down to the call room, just about to race, and again Bill dragged me to one side and said, 'I want you to go out fast.' I thought, 'Crikey, we've been here before mate, this is bizarre.'*
>
> *This time though, I'd learned from the experience and I was confident in my own race plan. I took it on-board and just gave him a polite nod, but stuck to my race. This time I got into the final. And although I just missed out on a medal by a couple of hundredths of a second, the most important thing was that I could stick to my race plan.*

It Tastes Bad . . . but Does you Good

Those really powerful experiences often give rise to the biggest changes. We learn the most from them. As we worked together over the years, Chris and I became aware that the learning opportunities were always there. They are there in every single day of everybody's life. Sometimes we take them and make the most of them, we recognize them and we use them. Sometimes they pass us by. Personally, I think that's one of the key differences between world-class people and the rest. They absolutely grab every learning opportunity. They recognize that some learning opportunities come with hurt. There is an emotional impact that can accompany failure. Therefore, a lot of people will try and forget those moments. They might try to put the moment behind them and forget it. Well, maybe the idea is not to forget the moment. Maybe the idea is to use it to help make them stronger as a result.

"I try to learn from mistakes very quickly. I think it's important to get back on the horse and carry on . . . I know that I will be in some pain and discomfort but it will be worthwhile."

Bruce Duncan, Team GB captain and
world-leading adventure racer

"

Learning Requires Responsibility

Chris Cook describes another experience in 2005, which became a catalyst that sparked change.

I got up onto the blocks one year at the European Championships, tipped to win it. The whole place went silent. The next noise I hear is the fire alarm going off. I thought it was the gun. I dived in and everyone else stood down. You're only allowed one start in swimming so I was out (disqualified). That was me done.

I got out the water, chatted to my coach and a couple of my team-mates and they all said, 'Oh Cooky, you were ever so unlucky there mate'. My first reaction was, 'No, I could have controlled that better, the rest of the competitors did.'

You have to look around and see who is surviving in the environment and what they're doing to respond differently. You have to search pretty deep, and that's what we had to do.

"

As we can see in this account, Chris made decisions to do things differently. He challenged himself harder and pushed his own boundaries further. It is these challenges which extend our capabilities.

Challenges that truly extend us are the ones that help us to make significant steps in our growth and development. Sometimes these challenges are set for us or imposed by circumstance. Sometimes we take them on when they arrive. Sometimes we might shy away from them. Those who have reached the very top of their field seem to not only take on challenges when they are presented, they actually seek them out. By seeking out these challenges, they deliberately enter virgin territory. Often these people do not know exactly what they will encounter, or what challenges they will face. As Ben Saunders said, he often has no idea how he'll overcome the challenge when he sets out. For many people, this might seem a daunting or even scary prospect.

Uncertainty is One Thing You Can Count on

These accounts show how highly successful people voluntarily enter a state of 'not knowing'; that is to say, uncertainty. Ironically, many people actively avoid uncertainty because of the angst that often accompanies it; they see it as a threat. However, proven winners do not seem to take the same view. Perhaps it is because uncertainty is normal to them. They spend so much of their time pushing the boundaries. Maybe they actually relish the uncertainty because it provides them with opportunities to extend themselves and become better at what they do. I suspect that they are stimulated and excited by the prospect of navigating the uncharted territory. Added to this, they have the confidence of having stepped into the unknown many times in the past, and therefore have the knowledge that they can survive. In reality, the future is always uncertain, no matter how much certainty we think it may have. In that case, we simply have to choose how we perceive it and respond to it.

During his career, gold medal-winning swimmer Chris Cook actively sought opportunities to step outside of his comfort zone to push his own personal boundaries. One such example was a competition that Chris entered in Eastern Europe. Chris chose to enter the meet *because* it was difficult to get to and he knew he'd be staying in very modest accommodation. Chris also knew he would be competing in a cold pool against some very fast, keen, young Eastern European athletes who were in race condition. Chris, on the other hand, was in the middle of a heavy training cycle. Chris Cook deliberately created a significant challenge for himself. The purpose of the challenge was to help us to find any cracks in his approach, his preparation and his performance. We knew that we needed to expose the cracks before we could work on them. The principle behind this approach was simple. The demands of training had to be tougher than the demands of competition.

High achievers relish the opportunities to be pushed and to push themselves. Linda Conlon, Centre for Life's Chief Executive, understands that her team need to have the ability to push and be pushed.

> *"Good people have elasticity. They are good outside of their comfort zone. Textbook qualifications are not enough . . . the real world skills are crucial. In order to take opportunities, people need to be able to think outside of the box . . . good people normally go further when they're pushed."*
> **Linda Conlon, Centre for Life Chief Executive**

Where are the Boundaries Anyway?

How far do you push? Do you know where your limit is? I don't mean the point at which you become uncomfortable; I mean 'the limit'. Where is your ceiling? What is possible? Where is the line that separates 'possible but extremely difficult' from 'impossible'? How do you find that line? Where is the boundary?

World Barista Champion James Hoffmann understand the importance of knowing where his limit is in his coffee roasting business. James realizes that the best way to find the limit is to push something until it breaks. This approach is at the heart of his creative process. When James finds the breaking point, he can start to understand why it failed. This knowledge helps him to know where the true boundaries are and how to operate close to the edge. This is a skill that I've also noticed in motor racing drivers. In order to drive their car as fast as possible, they need to operate extremely close to the 'limit' of both their performance and the car's performance. If they push beyond the limit, they will crash. On the other hand, if they fail to drive close enough to the limit, they will be left behind.

James Hoffmann worked with a chef called Chris Young, who heads up the experimental kitchen at Heston Blumenthal's restaurant, The Fat Duck. He explained that their aim was to explore what could, and could not be done with coffee. In James' words, they 'made some colossal mistakes; some of the worst taste experiences of my life'. However in doing so, James and Chris found the limits and were therefore able to work within them more confidently. As far as James Hoffmann is concerned, this process is vital.

Interestingly, James does not only apply this mind-set to innovating with flavour combinations. He uses this same mind-set to innovate in business as well. James broke away from an industry standard when he began to market seasonal coffee. Knowing that coffee is harvested in crops every four to eight months, James decided to embrace seasonality and change. Each season, they produce a new espresso blend that provides the best of each individual crop. For the last few years, James' business, Square Mile Coffee, has produced a winter espresso, as well as a spring, summer and autumn espresso. As such, 'seasonal coffee' has become central to James' brand, and has been extremely successful. However, James knows that he must change it, because a lot of other roasters now market seasonal coffee too.

> *"Have you ever read a book called* The Red Queen*? It basically states that any evolutionary advantage is lost very quickly. If you run faster you find that eventually the slow ones die out and you're left only with the other fast runners; so you're left with no advantage. So, any advantage you gain is temporary. You see many, many, many businesses that come into the market with their one great idea and they think that's it, the game's won. But in reality that simply doesn't happen."*
> **James Hoffmann, World Barista Champion**

Despite 'seasonal coffee' being a central part of the brand, James' next steps for the business involve trying to fix an issue thrown up in creating this seasonal brand. There is an expectation that 'winter espresso' will taste like Christmas and that 'summer espresso' will taste like a summer meadow. Of course, this is not the case. As James explains, coffee is grown in the tropics, which don't have a spring, summer, autumn and winter. Therefore, James is now focused on disconnecting each crop from our seasons, and re-connecting it to the harvests. In his words, James wants to 'fix the problem that we created'.

> *"Despite it being the thing that people associate with us most, it's the thing we're going to drop. We need to find a new way of describing it. It's great that people enjoy the evolution but we found a way of creating confusion and we need to fix that. It does feel like we're about to 'kill the golden goose' and make a 'new Coke' mistake here, but I don't think we are."*
> **James Hoffmann, World Barista Champion**

I find James' decision-making process fascinating and inspiring. His seasonal coffee brand provides 85% of his turnover and 90% of his profit. How many other businesses would 'kill-off' their golden goose' because they knew that it wasn't quite right yet? James has a very successful product and brand. He's not proposing to scrap it because it has some critical flaw and is failing miserably. However, he is willing to get rid of his seasonal brand because he knows that it can be better, and because he understands the importance of staying ahead of the evolutionary curve.

Courage

James' account raises an awful lot of interesting and very important issues. He recognizes that in order to be innovative and creative, we must push the envelope and that ultimately we must be willing to fail. In order to find where the boundaries are, we must be willing to push hard enough to reach them. This often requires courage. In his book, *The Courage to Create*, Rollo May (1975), explains how creative acts often require great courage on a number of levels. Often when we create something new, we have to abandon something; destroy it. Many scientists do this with theories that they disprove through their creative acts of research. The theories that they destroy or abandon are actually a place of comfort. They provide familiar territory for the scientist. Those theories may have been the source of their professional reputations. Throwing those away or departing from that familiar ground requires great courage. Often the new territory that we're exploring contains many unknowns. Creative acts require us to leave what we know and journey into the unknown. They often require us to 'kill-off the golden goose', as James describes it, and take a huge leap of faith. We are required to choose a state of limbo, over what we know. And what makes world-leading people and organizations do this? It seems that they simply know, that what they have is not quite right yet.

England Squash's Head of Performance Keir Worth knows that the recipe that has kept England at the top of the world for the last 15 years will not keep them there. He realizes that they must change. In recent years, Keir and his team have become aware that there are new challenges which they need to respond to. Changes in the social and cultural landscape mean that it is more difficult to attract athletes into squash in the UK. Becoming an elite squash player requires a great deal of time and travel, which often means the families of junior players go to extreme lengths. It is an expensive pursuit. As a consequence, many athletes drop out of the system. This makes life more challenging for Keir and his team. In addition, countries such as Egypt, Malaysia and India have greater resources and less social pressures. Children in Egypt play squash for a vast number of hours from the age of five. England Squash cannot copy the Egyptian model, so they need to produce a model that works.

> *"It would be easy to say, 'Well of course Egypt will produce great players, they start playing at five years old', but that doesn't get you anywhere."*
> **Keir Worth, England Squash's**
> **Head of Performance**

Therefore, Keir and his team have been pushing the envelope in other ways. England Squash are focused on building on a traditional strength, coaching. Keir is currently working to make coaching more effective, so that each coaching session gives the players more benefit. He explains that coaches need to be able to engage players more effectively. It is not enough to simply deliver tactical knowledge and technical skills training. Keir knows that coaching also needs to impact upon players and inspire them. Coaching requires greater engagement, intensity and leadership. Therefore, England Squash are educating coaches to appreciate the individual differences in each player, such as their learning style, personality type and traits. As Keir knows, this is a massive cultural change and one that requires a great deal of effort.

Personally, I applaud England Squash's approach. They have dominated the world of squash for decades and yet they refuse to rest on their laurels. Keir Worth describes it as a 'relentless inquisitiveness', the drive to learn more and be better. The ability to do this through critical self-reflection is common amongst the highly successful people I interviewed. By pushing and failing, they expose weaknesses in their own game. These people are willing to ask and answer the really tough questions. Even though many of them are already ahead of their competition, they keep pushing themselves in the full knowledge that they are likely to fail.

'I Have Failed Far More Times Than I Have Succeeded'

The accounts from our world-class people are incredibly revealing. They are not afraid to push their boundaries and work outside of their comfort zone. They know that they are likely to fail. They understand that they will invariably make many attempts before they get it right. Sometimes it will take literally hundreds of hours of work, years of practice. Unlike many people, they embrace the opportunities. I asked polar explorer Ben Saunders what he felt his biggest lesson had been to date:

"Not being afraid to set big goals. If I know how I'm going to do it, the challenge is not hard enough. Not to be afraid of failure. I have failed far more times than I have succeeded."

So, mistakes should not be seen as an inconvenience; they are incredibly valuable! You should therefore seek out those challenges. Look for opportunities to be stretched, or to stretch the people around you. Accept the need to change and innovate, even if this means abandoning what you know or the very things that have made you successful in the past. Inevitably, you may find that the process is uncomfortable. Often it requires a great deal of effort and soul searching. Simply put; it's tough. Pushing your envelope invariably requires you to be tough!

Summary

- Pushing the boundaries inevitably means that you'll make mistakes and fail.
- In order to find the limit, we need to push hard enough to find the breaking point.
- Sometimes we need to abandon what we know and venture into the unknown.
- Failure can actually be a catalyst to success if you use your experiences to the full.
- Seek out the opportunities to extend yourself beyond your comfort zone!

6
Be Mentally Tough

In order to push the envelope, we often need courage. We need the courage to push ourselves, operate outside of our comfort zone and to risk failure. As these world-class performers have shown us, the journey to reach the pinnacle requires us to take on tough challenges, face ourselves, engage in serious soul-searching, ask the tough questions and find the answers. It is not a journey for the faint hearted. It requires mental toughness.

Mental toughness, mental strength, resilience and tenacity are terms that are regularly used in the world of elite sport. As sport psychologist and researcher Michael Sheard (2012) suggests defining these terms is a challenging task in its own right. In his 'Mental Toughness Code', Dr Sheard proposes that mentally tough athletes know how to win, they have the courage to stand tall in the face of adversity and refuse to be intimidated. In his words, 'Mental toughness is the stuff of champions.' The term, mental toughness, tends to incorporate a combination of traits such as a winning mentality, work ethic, self-confidence, motivation, attitude control and positive energy. Many other sport psychologists, coaches and athletes have also commented on the importance of mental toughness, suggesting that it is often *the* defining difference between the very best and the rest in sport.

"They are relentless. They won't give you anything. They have that desire to never give in, that refusal to give in."
Keir Worth, England Squash's
Head of Performance

Keir recognizes that the very best squash players in the world are physically and mentally tough. In particular, Keir points to examples such as world number one, Nick Matthew. Although Nick has a great technical and tactical game, Keir acknowledges that he is really tough mentally.

What is Mental Toughness?

But what is this phenomenon we call mental toughness? England Squash's Keir Worth and National Head Coach Chris Robertson highlight the need for elite players to cope with, and thrive under, the pressures that the game imposes upon them. Tougher players are often able to produce their very best performance in 'high pressure' moments. As a former world number two, Chris Robertson also emphasizes the need to perform during periods of adversity, particularly in situations where 'the chips are down' and players find that they have their 'backs to the wall'. All players will experience tough situations; injuries, poor form, playing on foreign shores in front of a partisan crowd. In those situations, Chris and Keir look for players who are able to separate their inner world (their thoughts and emotions), from the outer world (their environment). They observe players and notice how they respond to tests. How do the players react? Who backs off? Who pushes on?

These accounts highlight a number of elements to mental toughness, such as ability to keep going through adversity and the ability to bounce back, which is sometimes referred to as resilience. Both of these are key elements for those who aspire to achieve in sport.

You have to be tough to be successful in many walks of life. Twice Michelin-starred chef Kenny Atkinson knows that there are times when chefs feel under pressure or below par, and when they are tempted to give up or back off. In these situations, some people may produce a below par performance. However, others are able to knuckle down and perform anyway. The tougher chefs are also willing to make the sacrifices that others don't seem to be willing to make. Another very important trait of the mentally tough is the ability to take a leap of faith and believe in yourself.

> *"It's the ability to not give up, even when every bone in your body is screaming at you to stop."*
>
> **Bruce Duncan, Team GB captain**
> **and world-leading adventure racer**

Before writing this book, my definition of mental toughness was limited to my view of it in a sporting context. Often I would see athletes or teams encounter an adverse situation, or a challenging question. Some would stick to their game plan and keep performing. Others would fold, and in doing so, they would throw the game plan out of the window. Initially, I saw mental toughness as the ability to keep executing the game plan, whatever happens. Obviously, our game plan needs to be agile and adaptable. It needs to account for changes in circumstance. However, we should not panic and discard it when we encounter challenges.

So now, after interviewing these exceptional people, my definition has broadened. In Chapter Two, retired US Navy SEAL Gary Rossi talks about 'staying on task' being a key component of mental toughness. That idea is very closely aligned to Alan and Bruce's view that mental toughness simply means 'not giving up'. And it is this element, *not giving up*, which I now believe is at the core of mental toughness.

Undoubtedly, there are points when giving up seems easier. Mountaineer Alan Hinkes, experienced this first-hand. As he reached the top of his 14th 8000-metre peak, Kanchenjunga, Alan found himself in a perilous situation. He was on his own, in the dark, and had been caught in a blizzard. His climbing partner had dropped back earlier on because it was getting dark, but Alan had decided to soldier on. He had made the decision to return in the dark, having done a lot of night climbing in the past. However, Alan knew the odds of returning alive were suddenly stacked against him. As he stood there alone and exhausted in the darkening blizzard, he remembered several friends who had previously died on Kanchenjunga:

> *"I thought I was joining them. I remember having a panic attack. I was shaking and hyperventilating. I'm not stupid. I reckon I am a realist. I have been climbing 30 years and I know what happens. I thought, 'This is for real Alan, you're going to die, there is no point in messing around and fooling yourself'."*

In this situation, I suspect many climbers would have concluded that the game was over. As a result, they may well have curled up and died on the mountain. Alan knew he had to focus to try and pull himself together, both mentally and physically. Rather than giving up, Alan decided to use all of his 30 years of experience to get off the mountain. He describes the way he focused everything into a pin-head, all of his energy, determination and experience.

> *"When I focused on trying to get myself out of that situation, I remember that there was no fear whatsoever, it was pure euphoria, pure nirvana, pure pleasure . . . it was real and it was absolutely amazing, yet it was serious climbing."*
> **Alan Hinkes, world-leading mountaineer**

An Extreme Challenge Needs Extreme Toughness

During the Easter of 2011, Bruce Duncan and his training partner Anthony, embarked on a mammoth athletic event called The Epic Tri.

We did the 42 peaks of the Lake District, covering 65 miles in 24 hours [a challenge known as the 'Bob Graham']. Then we went straight to John O'Groats [north eastern tip of Scotland] and cycled to Land's End [south western tip of England] on a tandem bike, non-stop. Then it was straight up to Devizes, then Westminster in the canoe, which is 125 miles.

I injured my left knee early in the run in the Lake District, within the first few hours of starting, and was hobbling most of the way. It was incredibly painful. At that point we had about six days left to go. I shifted some weight around in my bag to try to make it easier, but there was no way I was giving up.

We were on the bike for 78 hours. Towards the end I couldn't feel my neck or lift my head up. All I could do was look down between my arms and the handle bars to keep sight of the white line on the road. We ended up attaching a piece of string to my helmet so that my cycling partner, Anthony, who was on the back of the bike, could pull the string to lift my head up.

It was incredibly uncomfortable. Two and a half weeks after finishing the event, I still have numbness in my fingers and toes.

Enduring incredible discomfort seems to be par for the course when you're striving to become the best. Ultra-distance runner Andy McMenemy encountered a number of injuries during the 66 days of 'Challenge 66', but persevered nevertheless. On the second day, Andy injured his Achilles tendon. His ankle and Achilles were swollen, which made running an ultra-marathon difficult and extremely painful. At the time, Andy thought that was the most painful experience he would ever have to endure. That all changed on day 24, when he injured his tibialis anterior muscle.

After completing his run on day 27, Andy went to the local hospital to get a scan on the injured leg. Knowing that it was not fractured, Andy ran another ultra-marathon the following day. Although his times increased from six hours to around ten hours for the next few days, Andy went on to run all 66 ultra-marathons back-to-back.

> *"At one point I could not even bare the pain of an ice cube being placed on it. I thought the skin was about to burst open . . . the real problem though was not the pain but the thought that this might be a show stopper and that I might not be able to complete the challenge."*
>
> **Andy McMenemy, record-breaking**
> **ultra-distance runner**

Clearly, world-class people have mental toughness. As we can see, toughness can be expressed in many different forms. Mental toughness is often necessary when you're attempting a challenge that requires extreme physical exertion. The ability to keep going through physical discomfort and pain is a relatively obvious example of toughness. However, there are other dimensions to mental toughness. Sometimes our greatest challenges require us to face our innermost fears.

It's Not Just Physical

Mental toughness often requires us to dig deeper than we thought possible and trust ourselves to do something we doubt we can do. The real test is a test of belief, rather than physical endurance.

> ### To Quit, or Not to Quit . . . That is the Question
>
> Mountaineer Alan Hinkes describes how the mental toughness required to climb the world's highest peaks often extends beyond the ability to merely push your body:
>
> *A lot of inexperienced people focus on the summit. On Broad Peak, there was a client who did just that and just focused on the summit. We tried to slow him down but it made him madder. He was going faster than me at one point and I kept thinking, 'Where is he getting his energy from?' We got to the top and he pulled out all his sponsor's flags. The whole time I was thinking that something was wrong, because the summit is not the end. You have to descend.*
>
> *As we went to leave the summit he could hardly move. We got him down to about an hour from the summit and he said, 'That's it, I just can't do it.' I said to him, 'Well if you stay here, you'll die, and I'm not staying with you, because if I do, I'll die. I'm going down and you're coming with me.'*
>
> *Eventually we made him realize that he had to carry on. However, if he hadn't had anyone else to help him along, he probably would have given up and died on that mountain. No doubt he had the drive to get to the summit, but you have to think about the bigger picture.*

You Have to Dig Deep

Polar explorer Ben Saunders explained that however physically challenging his polar expeditions may be, his biggest challenges are not physical.

To be honest, my sense of self-belief has been pushed far more than any part of me physiologically. It's when I have to deal with 'failure'. It's the ability to motivate myself during difficult times. It is more than just discipline. I need to be able to find my reason for carrying on. There have been many times when it seemed hopeless, when the odds were stacked against me. I have been broke. I have been at points where every avenue seemed to have petered out. Invariably, that's when things seem to happen.

I have a real distain for the word 'impossible' now. There are times when you really have no option but to keep going. It actually helps when you get to those 'brick wall' moments. You have to have utter commitment.

James Hoffmann also recognizes that toughness is required during a barista competition. Although making and serving coffee does not have a huge physical demand, there is still an element of toughness. Doing this on stage in front of thousands of people is a very different challenge to serving coffee in a café. In his experience, it can throw even the most experienced barista. Olympic finalist Chris Cook also appreciates the greatest challenges are not necessarily the physical challenges. Even in an athletic event, such as the 100-metre breaststroke, Chris knows that the greatest challenges are mental. He explained that the toughest test comes when he's positioned in lane four. The athlete in lane four is the favourite, because they qualified with the fastest time; they are expected to win.

"The only thing that can hold you back is what you tell yourself. That's the time when there is greatest pressure from the outside and potentially from the inside."

**Chris Cook, double Olympian and
Commonwealth champion**

How is Toughness Developed?

However it is experienced, there is very strong evidence telling us that mental toughness is crucial for those who want to be the best they can be. But how is mental toughness created? How is it developed? Is mental toughness something which is innate, or can it be nurtured through experience? Interestingly, in an autobiographical account of his experiences as a prisoner in Nazi concentration camps, Viktor Frankl (2004) noticed that the 'toughest' men were not the most physically robust, but the ones with inner fortitude. He explains that those with deep spiritual and moral foundations were the ones who could bear more suffering. Certainly these traits are unlikely to be innate.

Some of those who have studied the development of mental toughness in athletes have suggested that the environment is the pivotal factor. Through his studies of the world's sporting 'Gold Mines', Rasmus Ankersen (2011) noted that in many cases, the fierce competition gives rise to mentally tough athletes. In order to succeed in this incredibly competitive environment, athletes were forced to become tough. If you want to become a successful female golfer in South Korea, a female tennis player in Russia, a runner in Kenya or Egypt, you have to be tough enough to beat the thousands of others hoping to beat you to the dream. In Rasmus' words, there is a tiny percentage that 'pass through the eye of the needle'. The intensity of the training and competition dictates that only the toughest will make it. In Jamaica, promising athletes attend *the* school athletics championships, known as 'The Champs'. It is designed to be a 'high pressure' cauldron for the young athletes. 'The Champs' is the focus of the entire nation; the stadium is packed with 30,000 people, it is on television and on the radio. The thinking is simple. If a junior athlete can perform at 'The Champs' they will probably be able to perform anywhere.

> *"Toughness and resilience come through maintaining the standards, giving responsibility and making people accountable. There is no room for excuses."*
>
> **Kenny Atkinson, twice Michelin-starred chef**

Knowing the importance of mental toughness, Michelin-starred chef Kenny Atkinson works to develop it in his team. He deliberately fosters mental toughness in his team by ensuring that all of his chefs maintain high standards, take responsibility and are held accountable. Kenny explained that he learned to be mentally tough in exactly the same way. His head chefs made him accountable for upholding the standards of his work.

Highly successful people from vastly different domains have very similar views on the development of mental toughness. Mountaineer Alan Hinkes also emphasized the need for discipline, the need to uphold standards and to push people to take on tougher challenges. In developing the world's best players, Chris Robertson also described how England Squash demand a professional attitude, attention to detail and self-responsibility, because these are crucial in the development of toughness. Keir explained that historically, the demands of competition would develop toughness in players. Those players who learned to thrive in the competitive cauldron would be the ones to rise to the top. Nowadays, they cannot rely on the competitive framework alone. Like Kenny Atkinson, the team at England Squash are deliberately cultivating toughness in the players, through coaching and leadership.

> "It emerges through good coaches and what they do on a daily basis with players. Coaches create boundaries. They talk to players about what is acceptable behaviour and what isn't, on court and off court, and by developing players as professionals."
> **Keir Worth, England Squash's Head of Performance**

Interestingly, Chris Robertson and Keir Worth spend time observing athletes in training and competition. They look for players who have a consistent approach to every game, regardless of the situation, the circumstances, or the opponent. They will assess how players take on challenges and respond in critical moments. And whilst they do not expect the athletes to be perfect, both Chris and Keir are keen to ensure that the players learn from their experiences and become stronger as a result. Interestingly, there are common themes that run though all of these accounts: discipline, professionalism, accountability, responsibility and taking on ever-increasing challenges. These appear to be the fundamental building blocks upon which toughness is developed. By looking at these elements, it's clear to see many of the habits and traits that differentiate world-class performers from their peers. We have already identified that high achievers 'push the envelope' and therefore take on progressively tougher challenges. Taking responsibility is another key element that differentiates those who have reached the pinnacle of their field. These seem to be the very foundations upon which mental toughness is built.

Is It Really a Brick Wall?

The accounts of these highly successful people show us that we do not need to rely on a competitive environment. We can take many of the principles that they have shared, and apply them to ourselves. One of the fundamental steps is to push through the boundaries. You need to be able to continually challenge and push through your own limits. Team GB captain Bruce Duncan encourages members of the Wenger Patagonian Expedition team to keep pushing through their thresholds and is acutely aware that this is not something that can be taught in the classroom.

> *"You have to experience it. You have to find the limits. You have to have the stubbornness to keep pressing against the boundaries. Sometimes you don't know that you'll get through but for me, I have to keep pushing, I can't give up."*
> **Bruce Duncan, Team GB captain and**
> **world-leading adventure racer**

Runners often experience a point that is known as 'the wall'. It is the point where you feel like you have run out of energy and cannot go on. Record-breaking ultra-distance runner Andy McMenemy knows this feeling all too well, but understands that this wall is always psychological. Andy described the way he would have an internal dialogue, telling his body that he was taking control and that he was going to keep on going. Once he'd got through a threshold, he'd say 'see, I told you we could do it'. The wall becomes a mental block, and the only way to break through it is to take control.

> *"The wall is always psychological."*
> **Andy McMenemy, record-breaking**
> **ultra-distance runner**

It's a Hurdle, Not a Brick Wall

When retired US Navy SEAL Gary Rossi trained at BUDS (Basic Underwater Demolition/SEAL (BUD/S) School), he found himself pushing on the boundaries and going beyond the limit of what he thought was possible:

Most people stop when things get uncomfortable, not when they hit their limit. Most people don't actually know where their limit is, because they've never experienced it.

When I was training at BUDS, we used to do an exercise in the pool. They called it the training tank. The tank was 25 yards wide and in order to pass this one physical fitness test, you had to do a breath-hold of at least three widths. So that was about 75 yards underwater with one breath.

When you are swimming underwater and your body is working, you're experiencing oxygen deprivation. You probably have about three barriers that you have to get through where your body and mind says, 'you need air'. However, you have to tell your mind, 'you can make this'. I remember doing three and three-quarters or maybe even four widths underwater. There are three to four barriers where you start thinking, 'hey, I have to get a breath of air'. Then you say, 'no you don't, you've got some more, push yourself'.

Most people wouldn't know that there are three barriers, because they never cross the first one. And that's the difference that Gary's experience gives him. Most people don't realize that they are just hurdles. They don't understand that they can be crossed. Many would think that it's a brick wall and impossible to cross. They wouldn't appreciate there is life on the other side.

Why do They Push so Hard?

When reading these accounts, you may probably start to wonder why these people push themselves so hard. Why do they continually put themselves into positions where they encounter such challenges? Why do Bruce Duncan and Andy McMenemy endure the physical discomfort required to excel in ultra-endurance events? Why does Alan Hinkes accept the risk of death, and put himself in a position where he comes face-to-face with it? Why does Kenny Atkinson push himself and his team harder and harder to excel in the kitchen? What makes these people engage in the challenges that ultimately create this mental toughness?

There is a concept in psychology called *The Hardiness Construct* (Frankl, 2004), which has its roots in existentialism. Existentialists propose that *hardiness* provides us with the courage to pursue the future, despite its uncertainty. Rollo May (1975) recognizes that uncertainty often causes us to feel anxious because it is 'rootless'.

Rollo May explains that through uncertainty we experience the anxiety of nothingness. Researchers began to observe individual differences in people's reactions to the stress we experience in times of uncertainty and adversity. Those people who seemed to thrive and survive, tended to display three attitudes: commitment, control and challenge. Those who are committed feel deeply involved in their activities. The activities are integral to their lives. Therefore, those who are committed actively pursue, rather than withdraw. They pursue because they have an innate interest and love for the activity, no matter what challenges it presents. This level of commitment may well be born out of passion. Is it their dreams, passion and love for what they do, that drives these world-class people to delve deeper and deeper into the challenge? Is it this love, and the relentless inquisitiveness, that gives them the appetite to push further into the unknown? Does their incredible level of focus help them to stay 'on task', no matter what?

> *"Self-belief has to be greater and stronger than all of the questions that you get thrown at you. Constantly stick to what you need to do and don't compromise. If I wanted to test someone's mental toughness, I would definitely test their desire and their focus. That's what it comes down to."*
> **Chris Cook, double Olympian**
> **and Commonwealth champion**

Chris' statement gives us a great insight into why some people give up, and others don't. Those who give up may not have the clarity of focus and the passion for what they do. Their reason to keep going through the discomfort may not be strong enough. Those who give up may not believe that they can be successful. If they don't believe they have what it takes, they may well say, 'What's the point?' Those with the dream, the love, the passion, the focus and the belief will probably keep going, no matter how tough it gets.

In his book, *Man's Search for Meaning*, Viktor Frankl (2004) outlines his personal adversity during World War II, when he was captured by the Nazis. He was sent first to Auschwitz and then to the Türkheim concentration camp along with his mother, father, sister and wife. Whilst there, he experienced unimaginable adversity losing all of his family members and witnessing countless tragedies. However, it was this depth of adversity which caused him to discover his concept of 'the last of human freedoms'. He states that, 'Everything can be taken away from a man but one thing: the last of the human freedoms – to choose one's attitude in any given set of circumstances, to choose one's own way.' Frankl, a Viennese psychiatrist, spent time helping his fellow inmates to survive the camps. His method of psychotherapy, known as *Logotherapy*, proposes that 'despair' is 'suffering' minus 'meaning'. He and his fellow prisoners endured enormous suffering for many years. Those with a reason to live, a meaning and a purpose, were able to survive. Frankl noted that once a man lost his reason to live, he died very quickly. In his words, 'He who has a *why* to live, can bear almost any *how*.' Viktor Frankl goes on to explain that if we are unable to find the meaning in our suffering then we will end up experiencing despair. Arguably passion is a powerful source of meaning and enables these exceptional people to experience the suffering without the despair.

Giving up is not the result of failure, it is the cause.

Where is the Limit?

Human beings accomplish some incredible feats. On occasions, it is tempting to think of them as 'impossible', because they are right on the limits of our own frame of reference. However, I believe it's important to understand that these feats obviously were possible. In fact, they were made possible *because* somebody pushed their body, mind and spirit hard enough and far enough. In so doing, people literally turn the 'impossible' into the 'possible'.

> ## When We Have the 'Why', We Find the 'How'
>
> Gary Rossi understands that, as human beings, we are capable of extraordinary feats. Normally the only thing preventing us from achieving them is our belief and our willingness to push. Gary tells how his friend and colleague, Michael E. Thornton, displayed both toughness and courage in battle, when he risked his life to save Lieutenant Tommy Norris:
>
> *Mike was an engineman second-class in the Navy, during Vietnam.*
>
> *Mike and Tommy Norris were working with the South Vietnamese (SV) SEALs, who had a reputation for not being the best in land-navigation. The truth is, they got lost in there. Like typical blokes who don't ask for directions, they knew they were lost but kept on driving. They weren't supposed to come under any enemy fire whatsoever, and there were five of them.*
>
> *Anyway, because they were in the wrong place at the wrong time, they ran smack dab into a battalion of North Vietnamese Regulars. Of course a fire-fight ensued. The way Mike says it, when they realized they were getting over-run, they withdrew. He was running with two of the SV SEALs and looked round and said, 'Where's the Lieutenant?' One of the SV SEALs said 'Lieutenant dead, Lieutenant dead.'*
>
> *Now, our teammates are the most important thing in our lives. Since we operate in small units, we have to rely on each other. We have specific*

duties and responsibilities and if one of us goes down, that's a big hit for the rest of us. We never leave our comrades behind – we have never left a teammate and not got him back. So, Mike went back.

If I remember correctly, Mike got shot twice – in the shoulder and in the quadriceps. But he picked up Tom Norris. Tom got hit by a round in the back of his head, in the left-hand side. It's remarkable, but the round did not penetrate the skull and was deflected by the bone mass around the top of the skull, and came out just above his left eye. It basically blew his eye out.

So, Mike had been wounded twice and was carrying Tom Norris, running to the beach, before swimming for two hours to the rendezvous.

Mike knows that when you go into battle, you may not get out alive. Mike was thinking, 'I'm not going to leave a teammate of mine. And when I get him out, I am going to do everything I can to save myself and save him.' That's the type of mental tenacity that I'm talking about. The fact is, you can do things that most people would have no idea they could do; that their body can do, that their mind can do. They have no idea that their mind can overcome the things that their body will endure.

It's tempting to think that accounts like this are made possible because the people involved are in some way 'super-human'. In my experience, they will be the first to acknowledge that they're just like everyone else. I agree with them. We all have the potential to accomplish incredible feats. Some people have the courage to explore their true potential. They work to the limits of what is possible. Others may only explore a very small proportion of their potential, and only know a fraction of what they're capable of.

Summary

- Mental toughness is not just required for physical challenges. Sometimes the greatest challenges are tests of self-belief.
- Mental toughness is built on discipline, maintaining high standards, responsibility, accountability and the ability to continually raise the challenge.
- Push yourself through your limits – it can be easy to give up when you become uncomfortable.
- To push yourself into discomfort, you need a reason, a meaning and a purpose that is strong enough. Have the *why*, and you'll find the *how*.
- Giving up is not the result of failure, it is the cause.

7
Take Responsibility, Take Control

Mental toughness is underpinned by traits such as discipline, accountability and professionalism. In the previous chapter, several of our world-class people explained how mental toughness is developed through those facets. They are central to success, and go hand in hand with responsibility. Viktor Frankl (2004) makes an interesting point when considering the word 'responsible'. He shows that 'response-able' means that we are 'able to respond'.

Ultimately, world-class people know that the responsibility for their success and in some cases their survival, stops with them. World number three Alison Waters like most professional squash players, is self-employed. She is acutely aware that she is entirely responsible for her own performance and, as such, she needs to lead her own development and her own training programme. In recent years, Alison has become much more particular about how she trains and more aware of what she requires from her coaches. When she first turned professional, she allowed the coaches to lead; they would direct her training programme. Nowadays, Alison leads her own training and preparation programme.

"The coaches won't dictate what we work on, they will ask. It means that I don't turn up for a session for the sake of it, I really need to get something from it. The physiotherapist could give me endless amounts of programmes, but if I don't do them, I won't benefit."
Alison Waters, England International squash player

Taking responsibility has a tangible importance. In reality, Alison's success on court has a direct impact on her livelihood. Mountaineer Alan Hinkes knows that those who fail to take responsibility may pay the ultimate price. Although a rescue team may be able to assist mountaineers on some mountains, they simply can't help on the bigger peaks. In the Himalayas, there aren't any rescue teams, so mountaineers have to be self-sufficient. Realistically, helicopters are not an option above 6000 metres. When Alan climbs an 8000-metre peak, he's on his own. Therefore, he has always taken responsibility for getting himself to safety.

"You're on your own on the 8000-metre peaks and that's why I pushed myself to do them, because you're not artificially on your own, you're really on your own"
Alan Hinkes, world-leading mountaineer

It is Central to Performance

Australian sport psychologist Phil Jauncey (2002) considers that responsibility and accountability are central to performance. He has worked with many of Australia's leading sports teams, notably in cricket and rugby league. In his book, *Managing Yourself & Others*, Jauncey argues that many people suffer from a modern-day cultural disease; they believe that it's okay to fail, as long as they feel good about it. Rather than looking for ways to address the issues that are causing them to fail, they look instead for excuses. To sum up his point, Jauncey says, 'I believe very strongly that everything I do is my responsibility and therefore, if I do not like what I am doing I can change it'. So, as Phil Jauncey suggests, responsibility goes hand in hand with control and choice.

Record-breaking ultra-distance athlete Andy McMenemy explained that responsibility comes when he chooses to take on the challenge. No-one else made him run 66 back-to-back ultra-marathons. The tough tests are part of the territory and part of the challenge that he chose to experience. Polar explorer Ben Saunders also understands that responsibility and control go hand in hand. In 2003, he embarked on his second ever expedition across the Arctic Ocean. The first, which he attempted with a partner, ended unsuccessfully. Therefore, Ben decided to go it alone on his second challenge. In describing his solo expedition, he explained that, 'I had more control, because it was down to me.'

Adventure racer Bruce Duncan knows that when you're in the middle of nowhere, hours from civilization, mistakes can be costly. He knows that he is ultimately responsible for his own safety and that of his team. Although that might seem like a burden, Bruce also knows that total responsibility provides complete control.

> "The wonderful thing is that the whole race is in your control. You don't have any help, but you have total responsibility."
> **Bruce Duncan, Team GB captain and world-leading adventure racer**

A common thread emerges from all of these accounts. Responsibility is something that world-class performers relish. They appreciate that if they do not take responsibility, they will not have control. Rather than avoiding responsibility, and making excuses, they seek the opportunities to take it. In Olympic finalist Chris Cook's words, the word 'blame' should be eradicated.

> *"If it was easy, everyone would be doing it. I heard a saying that you 'grow through' tough times, not 'go through' them."*
> **Andy McMenemy, record-breaking**
> **ultra-distance athlete**

Responsibility and Learning

So, responsibility and control go hand in hand. If we fail to take responsibility, we are not in control. If we constantly look to attribute a failure to external reasons, we will never be in control of our performance. Once we assume responsibility, we put ourselves in the driving seat. We can now address the issues because we recognize that we caused them. With this mind-set, we start to be more open to criticism and we become more self-critical. We look for ways to learn and get better. We are happy scrutinizing our self and our performance, so we dig deeper to examine our weaknesses.

> *"It's a mixture of taking responsibility for what's just happened to you, then looking for the deeper lesson and taking it forward to make it work every single day."*
> **Chris Cook, double Olympian**
> **and Commonwealth champion**

Many people that I have spoken to seem to hold a misconception about world-class performers. They believe that those who have reached the pinnacle of their field do not have much left to learn. The perception is that once you reach a certain level, you become a teacher rather than a learner. Although he is one of the world's leading mountaineers Alan Hinkes certainly understands the importance of being open to learning, letting his ego go and being able to accept criticism.

"If you're too egotistical you won't learn and you'll die."
Alan Hinkes, world-leading mountaineer

Alan's statement applies equally to everyone. If we're not learning, growing and developing then surely we are shrinking and dying. In previous chapters we have seen that highly successful people are not afraid to push the boundaries, challenge themselves and fail. They realize that by extending themselves and making mistakes, they give themselves more opportunities to learn and develop. This is only possible because they recognize that they have complete responsibility for their performance and for their development. As Alan Hinkes suggests, they also need to live beyond their ego, to transcend the need to blame, and therefore be able to accept criticism. If a person's ego needs to be *right* or *successful*, they will tend to blame circumstances or other people, rather than take responsibility or criticism.

Ego Gets in the Way

Commonwealth champion Chris Cook learned the importance of humbleness when he first started training with other Olympians. When Chris first started to train at the Regional Performance Centre in Newcastle, he worked alongside a swimmer called Susan Rolf. Susan was an Olympian and European champion. Chris imagined that she would be treated like royalty, carried in on a throne and have fluffy towels at the end of her lane. The reality was far different though, and was actually something that inspired Chris.

Rather than being carried in on a throne, Susan was actually the first to arrive at the pool. She was the one who put the lane ropes in to prepare the pool for each session. In fact, the European champion didn't even have her own lane in the pool. She actually shared with eight or nine other swimmers. This experience had a huge impact on Chris Cook's understanding of the work ethic and mentality required to become a great athlete.

> *"Your work ethic shouldn't change. You shouldn't change the formula that gets you there. So working alongside world-class athletes like that was a real eye opener for me. It was a blessing at that moment in time."*
>
> **Chris Cook, double Olympian**
> **and Commonwealth champion**

The experience helped Chris realize that no-one else was going to do it for him. If he wanted to be successful, he had to do everything required to make it happen. Having worked for many years with Chris Cook, I noticed that he was constantly aware of the need to take responsibility for every single element of his performance. He explained that it has had a profound effect on his approach.

> *"When you take responsibility, something magical happens; you start to take control."*
>
> **Chris Cook, double Olympian**
> **and Commonwealth champion**

Recently I heard a swimmer telling his coach that he hadn't performed very well because the pool was cold. In a flash, the coach replied, 'What, just in your lane?' As I listened to this, I immediately started to consider how this simple message applies to us all. We could apply that analogy to business very easily, using the words *economic climate*, instead of *the temperature of the pool.* I have heard many business leaders blaming the recession for the performance of their business. However, there are others who refuse to blame. Instead they are focused on making their business as successful as possible despite the global economic situation.

Don't Leave It to Chance

Taking responsibility is critically important in developing world-class players. It is something that National Head Coach and former world number two Chris Robertson recognizes from his own days as a developing player. He works hard to ensure that this mentality is built into the fabric of their development programme and looks for players who are willing to evaluate and be self-critical. He learned the value of this when he was a player. He understands that there is no point in blaming anyone else, or finding excuses, because those approaches don't lead to success. Therefore, England Squash deliberately encourage players to become independent, self-sufficient and responsible for themselves.

The ability to be self-critical is common in many world-class athletes that I've worked with. They are acutely aware of how to develop their game and improve their performance. This approach is vital in professional squash. Squash is unlike many other professional sports. Even at world level, squash players don't have an entourage or support team. On many occasions, they will not have a coach with them. Therefore, players need to be self-reflective and accountable for both their performance and development on a daily basis. These attributes become crucial when players face their toughest challenges.

Knowing that self-responsibility is vital, the team at England Squash ensure that it is at the forefront of their talent selection and development process. Therefore, junior players are encouraged to start early. Although the coaches provide feedback and support, it is the player who is ultimately responsible for their own development. Chris looks for players who are able to evaluate their own game, understand the areas that require work and then address them. In so doing, players take control of their performance.

> *"After a loss, I don't like to hear a multitude of excuses and the reasons why they lost, or players blaming other factors. They have to take self-responsibility. I don't mind if the referee didn't do a good job, I can understand that. But I want them to see the responsibility they had for the loss."*
>
> **Chris Robertson,**
> **England Squash's National Head Coach**

The reality is that we do have ultimate control over our own performance. Some people choose to see that and others don't. The truth is that we have control until we choose to give it away. As Viktor Frankl (2004) suggested, it is our 'last human freedom'. His experiences as an inmate in Auschwitz taught him that a human can be stripped of their possessions, their clothes, their dignity and even their name (inmates were referred to only as a number), but they still have the ultimate choice of how to think and feel. This is a sentiment that I agree with very strongly. Our performance is entirely within our control because it emanates from our thoughts and feelings. No situation, or circumstance or person can impact your thoughts and feelings, unless you give permission. If you feel threatened or intimidated by someone else, it is because you have allowed them to intimidate you. Although it may be difficult, you could choose not to feel threatened. Despite his experiences at the hands of the Nazis in Auschwitz, Viktor Frankl chose not to feel hopeless. We have the ability to control how we think and feel through the power of choice. Therefore, we have ultimate control over our performance.

When We Blame, We Relinquish Control

Responsibility and control are inseparable. Existential psychologists, such as John Martin-Fischer and Martin Ravizza (1998), would argue that freedom and responsibility are bound together because we have choice. We may not choose our circumstances, but ultimately it is our choices concerning how we think and feel, which govern our lived experience. As human beings, we have both the freedom and responsibility to live a fulfilling life. We have both the power and responsibility to choose how we experience the world. In essence, the message is: if we are not happy with our lot, we need to change! This idea presents many people with a daunting prospect. It literally means that we are responsible for ensuring we lead a fulfilling life. If we look at our life with dissatisfaction, we have two choices. We can either recognize that we are responsible and therefore need to make some changes, or we can choose to blame. In blaming something external, we attempt to deceive ourselves. We try to hide behind the notion that our situation is the result of something outside of our control. I suspect that we do this to protect our ego. Our ego doesn't like to think we are at fault. Through our ego, we are likely to judge our self. This judgement usually stings. So, to avoid the discomfort, we often choose to find an excuse. We choose to ease the pain, rather than take responsibility.

This challenge is exacerbated if we're feeling low on confidence. If we perceive that we're failing, and we feel the sting of self-judgement, our natural tendency might be to turn to excuses and blame. If we feel that we're in a vulnerable position, the easiest and most comfortable option is to look to external reasons. Ironically, these are the times when it is most important to take responsibility. The times when our performance has dropped, and we are low on confidence, are the most crucial times to take control. Only when we take responsibility can we regain control. Only when we re-gain control can we start to turn around the performance.

The best way to restore confidence is to raise our performance. Confidence comes from evidence. It's hard to fool yourself into feeling confident by turning to excuses. Confidence builds when we know how to get ourselves out of a hole and turn our performance around. If we blame external circumstances, it's hard to see how we can turn our performance around. By definition, external circumstances are outside of our control. Those people who choose to blame, allow themselves to be beholden to 'luck'. They wait for a stroke of luck, or a moment of good fortune to change their situation. Psychologically, that's not a great place to be. By taking responsibility, we are no longer beholden to luck. We can start to change our own circumstances and create the life experience that we desire. With responsibility and control, we give ourselves the opportunity to become exceptional.

> *"I now have an incredible level of self-belief and optimism. If I work at things, things work out. Sometimes I do get over-optimistic, thinking I can fit more into a day than is reasonable.*
>
> *I can get frustrated with other people. I have started to realize my own potential and I know that I am no different than anyone else. I have worked for everything. It's why I have such a disdain for that word 'impossible' now."*
> **Ben Saunders, record-breaking polar explorer**

By taking responsibility, you have the power to make things happen. Ben's experience shows that this simple approach has allowed him to achieve things that many people would have considered 'impossible'. In many ways he is just like the rest of us. He wasn't born with super powers. Nor were any of the other people I interviewed. The fact is, they don't need super powers to achieve the extraordinary. Instead, they have an approach and a mentality, which sets them apart.

Summary

- You only have true control when you accept responsibility.
- Seek out and relish the opportunity to take ultimate responsibility and complete control of your performance.
- You cannot always control the situation. However, you will always have control over how you think, feel and respond to any situation. You have the power of choice.
- Be open to learning. Sometimes that means accepting that we're wrong.
- Taking responsibility might not always be easy. It is often uncomfortable!

8
Be Yourself

There appear to be a number of habits and traits that characterize highly successful performers. We have looked at the importance of taking responsibility, being mentally tough, pushing our boundaries, attending to details, not compromising on standards, being focused and remaining in the moment. These are all vital elements and contribute to world-class performance. But I believe there is one trait that underpins all others. It is the ability to know yourself and be yourself. Without this foundation, none of the others are truly possible.

The Foundation of Passion

Let's start with dreams, intrinsic love for what you do and passion. Many people do not follow their dreams because they do not honour them. Being true to our dreams requires us to be true to ourselves. Following our dreams requires us to be authentic, to know ourselves, to be ourselves and therefore, be true to who we are. In other words, to follow our own path. Throughout this book, we have seen that passion is a crucial ingredient. It provides the *why*, the reason, meaning and purpose. Passion and love for what we do are very strong and enduring motives. Without passion, we are unlikely to survive the challenges that accompany the journey. If we do not intrinsically love what we do, we are unlikely to devote the thousands of hours of dedication required to become a true expert. If we lack the genuine intrinsic love for what we do, it is more difficult to immerse ourselves in it and allow ourselves to get lost in the moment. Being absorbed in the task is critical in order to find 'The Zone' (as discussed previously in Chapter Two), and therefore, is a vital component of peak performances. Anybody who wants to truly shine obviously needs to perform at their peak consistently. However, as we have also seen, the ability to focus on each step and become absorbed in each step, is critical for development as well as performance. We need to focus on each step so that we can get the most from every moment. The athletes who get a fraction of a per cent more from every training session, of every day, become significantly better than their peers over the course of years. Focus follows interest. In order to be constantly interested and engaged in what we do, we need to have a love for it. We need the passion.

The Power of Passion

As we have also discovered, passion gives us that obsessive, relentless inquisitiveness, which drives us to become better. Olympian Chris Cook gives an insight into how this relentless drive to gain the tiniest of margins creates excellence in other Olympic sports. He recalls listening to one of the coaches from British Cycling. The coach described the way in which Olympic Champion and world number one Nicole Cooke and her team constantly search for ways to get an extra thousandth of a second from the bike. They look at the tiniest detail, such as the viscosity of various lubricants. Passion can drive us to search out these minute, subtle details, and to find another tiny gain.

Ask the Tough Questions . . . of Ourselves

Passion is clearly pivotal. This knowledge emphasizes the importance of honouring our dreams and in doing so, being true to ourselves. But, there is more to it than that. There is another dimension. Finding the extra few millimetres, fractions of a second, or tiny competitive advantage, often requires us to look deeply at ourselves. On numerous occasions, these highly successful performers explain that their journey involved 'soul searching', scrutinizing, asking tough questions and looking at themselves in the mirror. The very process of soul searching requires us to take a good hard look at who we are, warts and all. We have to look, knowing full well that there are likely to be some things we don't like very much. In fact, the knowledge that we will find the warts is the most powerful reason for looking. The issues we find must be addressed. The questions must be answered. The truth is we can either choose to resolve them or pretend they are not there. It's the same choice we face when we're driving the car and hear a clanking noise or see a light flash up on the dashboard. We can pretend all is well and hope it will go away, or we take it to the garage knowing it's likely to cost us. Inevitably, the problem doesn't just go away. If we don't address it, it gets progressively worse, until one day we have no option but to address it. High achievers constantly ask the tough questions and address what they find. In doing so, they self-reflect and therefore become self-aware. They develop self-knowledge. Their knowledge of self allows them to ask more tough questions, and therefore to find even more answers. Sometimes the greatest discomfort produces the greatest insights.

"In the depths of my despair, so shall I find the meaning of my purpose. For it is here, my shell that is Ego, cracks wide open. In this place man finds reflection in its purist form."
Viktor Frankl, 2004

We Must Push Ourselves

The world-class people featured in this book also share another habit. They develop self-knowledge by pushing their envelope. Arguably, we have to extend ourselves in order to learn about our true self. How can we know ourselves if we never explore our boundaries and limits? If we only work within our limits, we will have a very narrow view of our true self. Before explorers began charting the globe, a map of the world looked very different from the way it looks now. We now know that the Earth is spherical because we have extended our exploration into space. If we apply that mentality to the knowledge of our true self, we can see why it is important to push ourselves through our boundaries. Only by exploring our limits and entering uncharted territory are we able to get an accurate picture of who we are. The very process of pushing ourselves through boundaries gives us confidence that we can push. As we continually take on new challenges, we start to believe that we can extend ourselves. The experience of doing it builds that confidence. As Ben Saunders says, we start to realize that our perception of 'impossible' is largely governed by self-belief. Conversely, if we fail to take on new challenges, and stick rigidly to our comfort zone, we start to believe that those things we can't currently do are 'impossible'. We create solid boundaries in our mind, separating us from those things we can't yet do.

Self-Belief Comes From . . . ?

Self-belief it seems, is also a critical component in this equation. It is something that characterizes those who are among the very best in their field. We need self-belief in order to push ourselves to our limits. During Chapter Six, we discovered that self-belief is a foundation of mental toughness.

"Self-belief has to be greater and stronger than all of the questions that you get thrown at you."

**Chris Cook, double Olympian
and Commonwealth champion**

How can we believe in ourselves if we do not know our true self? How can we have faith in something we don't know or trust? If we are to have self-belief, it stands to reason that we need to know who we are, be who we are and be true to who we are. These go hand in hand. If we cannot be ourselves, we will never know our self. If we are constantly portraying ourselves as something we are not, it is very hard to know, trust and therefore to believe in, who we are. In fact, the reason we try to create a façade in the first place is probably because we're not happy with ourselves. Those who are happy with themselves are happy to be themselves and have no need for the façade. If we're not happy with ourselves, how can we expect to have self-belief? Therefore, I consider that being yourself is central, and underpins many of the other characteristics that these highly successful people display. When chef Kenny Atkinson went on the televised competition, *Great British Menu*, he realized how vital it was to be just himself.

"It was the first thing that [judge] Nigel Haworth told me, 'Just be yourself and let your cooking do the talking.' He was right. You have to look yourself in the mirror afterwards."

Kenny Atkinson, twice Michelin-starred chef

Adventure racer Bruce Duncan realizes that his decisions and choices are driven by his desire to be the best he can be.

Inevitably this means that he is not likely to fit in with the crowd. He has been on stag weekends without drinking alcohol; he often makes choices of what to eat, where to eat and what to drink, that don't fit in with the majority. Bruce openly recognizes that consequently, many people will perceive that he's stubborn and selfish.

"I am not easily led. You have to know yourself to be happy to take your own path."

Bruce Duncan, Team GB captain
and world-leading adventure racer

World squash number three Alison Waters recognizes the need to be happy with who she is and comfortable being herself. Earlier in her career, she used to worry about who was watching and what they were thinking. A few years ago, the England team lost out at the World Team Championships. They were expected to win, and became caught-up under the pressure of this expectation, wondering what people would think if they didn't win. As a result, the team's performance was affected.

"I am not bothered about who is watching or what they think, particularly. If you start thinking those things you don't get anywhere."

Alison Waters, England international squash player

Many people will find that they compromise their authentic response. If Bruce were to give in to pressure from his mates and get drunk on the stag weekend, he might compromise his training. In doing so, he might allow himself to be pulled away from doing what was truly important to him. Life often tempts us to compromise our authentic response. We might not say what we truly believe, because it doesn't fit with those around us. We might temper our opinion because we feel that brutal honesty might make us unpopular. Maybe we think that being honest would get us fired. Perhaps we compromise our authentic response to appease somebody or simply for a quiet life. Life throws us many opportunities to either be true to our authentic response, or to compromise it.

Being Authentic

Alison's account illustrates that we are often drawn away from being ourselves. We are often tempted to create a façade in the belief that we will impress or appease others. Sometimes we are conscious of other people's expectations or judgements. We might try to change who we are, or mould ourselves to fit with other people.

> "Other people often comment when I am out on a trail that I'm a down-to-earth mountaineer. I don't put on any airs and graces, I'll just talk to anybody . . . I am happy being me and I might as well be because I can't be anyone else."
> **Alan Hinkes, world-leading mountaineer**

Authenticity requires us to be ourselves and be true to our self. If we're overly concerned about what others think, we're less likely to be true to who we are. In sport, athletes often fail to perform to their full potential because they feel pressure when they perceive that there are expectations on them. They start to focus on the expectations and the judgement that others will have of them if they 'fail'. Normally, when athletes focus on the outcome, they stop focusing on delivering the process and the performance falls apart. They become inhibited and some simply freeze up. It is a phenomenon that is true of both junior athletes and senior professionals. During an interview with BBC Sport, England soccer veteran, Jamie Carragher (2011) said that the England team have a fear of failure. He explains that the players are scared of making mistakes because of the reaction they will get from the press:

> *"The intensity of the press does get to the players," said the 33-year-old. "Sometimes I think players would prefer the press guy to think they had played well, rather than the manager."*

If the players are focused on trying to impress others, they will not be focused on playing the game. As a sport psychologist, I often see athletes failing to perform to their potential, because they are concerned about meeting expectations. Their mind is so tied up with concerns over the results, that they are not able to focus on the process.

> *"You have to fall in love with the process. You have to know the 'why', and when you do, the 'how' will come. Why do you want to do it? Why is it important? Is it admiration or respect from others? No. Is it integrity, because I said I would do it? Partly, yes. But I don't have to win the race to enjoy ultra-marathon running. I just come alive with the excitement."*
>
> **Andy McMenemy, record-breaking ultra-distance runner, on the importance of connecting with the process**

If you are able to focus on the processes, you stand a far greater chance of performing at your peak. Our focus follows our interest. Therefore, it helps to have an intrinsic interest and love for those processes.

What's the Real Reason?

In my work as a sport psychologist, I have noticed that those who are driven by a need to impress others are also likely to fall into another trap. They tend to try too hard. As we discussed in Chapter Three, there is a negative spiral that can start to develop when we try too hard, think too much and over-analyze. Inevitably we begin to lose our focus on the processes, and become drawn by our own negative thoughts and our worries that we will fail. The cycle deteriorates, causing us to make more mistakes and become more frustrated.

The obvious point here is that highly successful performers embrace mistakes; they do not fear them or avoid them. The accounts from those interviewed in this book show that they are happy making mistakes. They do not fear failure. They do not require a perfect outcome. They are not focused on impressing other people or looking for recognition. Therefore, they are happy to try and fail. Their ego does not crumple when they hit those tough challenges or when they need many attempts to achieve success. I believe that they are able to take on the challenges and make the mistakes because they know themselves, and are happy with themselves. They do not need the result in order to satisfy their ego or build their self-worth. Perhaps they don't fear failure because they are not trying to prove anything. They are happy trying and failing because they are motivated to engage in the task for its own sake, not because they need a perfect outcome.

The Trapdoor

When people find that the outcome holds importance for them, it is often because they want other people to accept them, to respect them or to be impressed by them. The outcome becomes vital because it is a means of generating self-worth. I believe that is a very fragile situation to be in. If we need a result or outcome in order to feel good about ourselves, we are likely to feel 'pressure', which can undermine our performance. Perhaps more importantly, we also need to realize that if we need a result or outcome to feel good, it means that we may have a hole in our self-worth that we're trying to fill. If we're looking to other people for acceptance, we are probably not providing it for ourselves. As Irv Blitzer (the character played by John Candy in the movie *Cool Runnings*) said, 'Gold medals are nice, but if you're not good enough without one, you will never be good enough with one.' Arguably the same could be said for fast cars, flashy watches, fancy job titles and big houses. If we are fuelled by the need for an outcome, or a result, or recognition, we are unlikely to have the passion needed to reach our full potential. Passion, as we have seen, is not driven by a desire for external rewards. It is driven by intrinsic forces, our love for what we do and the burning desire to be as good at it as we possibly can be. The years of dedication required to get to this level can only be fuelled by a powerful and stable motive. If we rely on external motives, such as results, rewards, outcomes and recognition, we are likely to see them wane when we hit tough times. Equally, those people that are driven by a need to succeed, often stop when they feel they've 'made it'. In Chapter One, we discovered that this holds true for athletes such as Ronaldo, Ronaldinho and Marat Safin, who became world-class as a means of escaping poverty. When the hunger dried up, so did the performance.

Throw Yourself into It

We have seen that those who have reached the pinnacle of their discipline did so by pushing the boundaries. They allow themselves to be creative and innovative. They are happy to break the mould and try something new. Creativity, as we have discussed, also requires courage. In Chapter Five, we discussed the need to have the courage to step way outside your comfort zone in order to innovate. This requires us to embrace mistakes, rather than get upset by them and avoid them. However, psychologist, Rollo May (1975) believes there is a deeper courage required to be truly creative. He argues that creative acts are based on an encounter between a person and their world. Creativity comes from within us, as a response to something in our world. It may be a problem that we're trying to solve. Or, like artists and scientists, we might be trying to make sense of something that doesn't quite make sense yet. Therefore our self is involved.

For great creative acts, Rollo May proposes that the encounter requires intensity and commitment. We need to throw ourselves into it completely. We must be wholly involved. We need to be engaged with real purpose. In order to do this, we have to be comfortable with who we are and to know who we are. The creative act exposes us because we have to throw our entire self into it. Those who don't know themselves tend not to commit fully to anything. Instead they keep something in reserve, hidden, guarded. Many people are like this in their relationships with others and with themselves. They never truly commit. If you wish to truly shine, arguably you need to commit fully. When people say that they throw everything into the task, they are referring to committing their entire self.

"I find that if I have a passion for something, I put my whole heart and soul into it."

**Kenny Atkinson,
twice Michelin-starred chef**

Perhaps it's also true that when we love something enough, we're happy to throw our whole heart and soul into it.

All These Words Start With 'Self'

Fully committing ourselves arguably takes courage. It requires mental toughness. In the previous chapters we looked at some of the elements that underpin mental toughness. When talking about mental toughness, many of those interviewed mentioned 'self-discipline', 'self-responsibility' and 'self-sufficiency'. These are important foundations, and interestingly all have a fundamental core; the first part of each word is 'self'. In fact, it could be argued that developing self-discipline, responsibility and self-sufficiency require that we look inward and look at ourselves critically. The process of critical self-reflection and evaluation is at the heart of developing self-knowledge. As we have already discussed, that process both requires and develops courage, a trait that we consistently see in the accounts in this book.

It is clear that these proven winners display enormous courage. But where does it come from? What is it that allows them to push themselves as hard as they do? What is it that allows them to enter the unknown? Why are they happy to take themselves deep into the land of uncertainty? How can they push through barriers, not knowing what lies on the other side? Is that something that they are born with, or have they developed it?

Where is the Limit Really?

It seems that there are two possible answers. Firstly, they have the belief that whatever happens, they can handle it. They have pushed barriers before and survived. Some of them have pushed too far, which helps them to know where 'too far' is. Even when they have pushed too far, they have still survived. The knowledge that you can push and survive is invaluable.

This Time He's Gone Too Far

Adventure racer Bruce Duncan knows that his true limit is not the point at which he becomes uncomfortable. By pushing to 'breaking point', he understands where his true limits really lie. This allows him to work to his maximum when he has no external reference points. Some people find that if they are racing head-to-head, they will work harder than they would with no competition. The competition drives them harder than they would tend to drive on their own. Bruce Duncan has learned not to rely on that external point of reference, so has to push himself to *his* limit.

> *I remember having hypothermia once, because I didn't eat and drink enough in one race. I also got heat exhaustion in Abu Dhabi in a 40-plus degree heat with no shade. The team had to carry me. Basically I got cooked in the middle of a desert. Sometimes you can push too hard.*
>
> *[...] In adventure racing, you don't know where the opposition is. They could be ahead of you or just behind you, or hours behind you. On a coast-to-coast race, I remember I had to push myself physically to make sure I kept my speed up. I didn't know where the others were, so I couldn't back off at any point. The only choice was to keep pushing harder and harder. I thought I needed to be about ten minutes ahead of the closest rivals going into the final stage, because I thought I'd lose time on it. So I really pushed the first two stages. In the end I won by about 45 minutes, but I couldn't back off at any point. That's probably the hardest I've pushed physically.*

Bruce knew that he could push himself that hard. He understood the difference between discomfort and his true limit. This gives him cast-iron confidence that he can produce his best performance whenever he needs to.

Back to Our Foundations

This incredible self-belief as discussed can only exist if we know who we really are. However, self-belief is probably not the only component. The other is likely to be passion.

> *"Courage is not the absence of fear, but rather the judgement that something else is more important than fear."*
> **Ambrose Redmoon**

Passion gives us that 'something else', which is more important than the fear. Alan Hinkes' passion for both the mountain and for living, could have been that *something* that made him keep going at the summit of Kanchenjunga, when he thought he was going to die. As his accounts illustrate, many other mountaineers in that position just give up. Bruce Duncan also explains that his mental toughness, his drive to keep going and not give up, is partly fuelled by his overwhelming desire to achieve the goal. It could also explain why Gary Rossi's colleague, Michael E. Thornton, went back into a battle to rescue his Lieutenant. Is it possible that saving his teammate was more important than the risk of losing his own life? I can relate to this idea personally. There are some things that are far more important than fear. Most people would agree that they'd risk their own lives to save their children or loved ones. They understand that there can be *something* that is far greater than the fear.

The power of passion in this situation can dwarf the power of external motives. We are more likely to do things we're truly passionate about in the face of fear, rather than do something for an external reward. Would Bruce Duncan or Alan Hinkes push themselves as hard if their motives were driven by external reward, rather than a passionate love for what they do and an internal drive to achieve their goal?

> *"If you want to do something, it's not impossible. If the 'why' is there, you'll find the 'how'. How are you going to do it? The plan has to evolve, it's not just going to be there. Be inspired by the question, 'Am I the kind of person that could do it?'"*
>
> **Andy McMenemy, record-breaking**
> **ultra-distance runner**

The accounts of our world-class people highlight the critical importance of passion and intrinsic love for what they do. They also illustrate the gravity of self-knowledge and authenticity, being true to who we are. My own experience tells me that authenticity and passion go hand in hand, and that being true to yourself is integral to understanding and recognizing your passion.

In My Experience

As I reflect back over my life, my successes and my failures, I can start to see that my failures have often followed those times when I have not been true to myself. I am sure that those close to me will have watched my moves with furrowed brows, and asked why I had decided to venture down a path which was not *me*. They will no doubt have asked themselves why I was embarking on a new business venture that didn't reflect who I am. Perhaps I was exploring my boundaries too, exploring the possibilities. Perhaps I needed to go down the path so that I could know it was the wrong one for me. Maybe you have to go down a dead end to know what a dead end looks like. My experiences have taught me to know who I am, to recognize my path, to understand my passion and honour it!

Does any of this resonate with you?

Summary

- It's hard to develop self-belief, self-discipline, self-responsibility or self-sufficiency (or any other word starting 'self-'), without really knowing *your*self.
- Passion is the enduring motivational force that will fuel your level of success. To be passionate, you need to be true to yourself.
- You have to know yourself and be yourself, in order to be true to yourself. This is fundamental if you want to follow your own path, your dreams and passion.
- Life will often tempt you to compromise your authentic response.
- When you are true to yourself and your passion, you're able to fully commit.

9
Be The Best You Can Be

So how can you become truly exceptional? One answer is; do what exceptional people do. Often it seems, these high achievers simply do things that other people do not. They make sacrifices that others are not willing to make. They push themselves harder than others are willing to push. Their accounts so far have already shown us many of the traits that set them apart. Many people would argue that success is largely down to a combination of innate talent and luck. Have these people been blessed with some innate gifts? Were they born with greater potential than the rest of us? Were they simply destined to become great or did they get lucky breaks?

Talent and Luck

These questions have been debated quite extensively throughout history. During the last few years, a number of best-selling books have been written on the subject of talent. Geoff Colvin (2008) explores the concept of talent in his book, *Talent is Over-rated*. Using a wide variety of examples, from disciplines such as sport and music, Geoff Colvin identifies a number of common foundations to expert performance. Firstly, he concludes that expert performance in any domain is usually developed over a period of more than ten years; it does not happen by chance and it is not developed overnight. Many truly expert performers started learning their discipline at a relatively young age. One example that Colvin cites, is that of a pair of young Hungarian girls who were 'schooled' to become Chess Masters. Their father wanted to discover whether talent in chess was innate. Neither the father, nor his wife, were chess players so he knew that any chess playing ability the girls developed would not come from genetic gifts. Following years of extensive practice and study, the girls went on to become world-class players. This example and many others suggest that expert performance is developed through thousands of hours of deliberate practice. Colvin, and others such as psychologist Karl Anders Ericsson, suggest that around 10,000 hours of deliberate practice is a prerequisite for expert performance. Daniel Coyle (2009) suggests that his book, *The Talent Code*, can be summed up in two words: practice better. After travelling the world to understand why certain places on Earth consistently produce world-class athletes, Rasmus Ankersen (2011) emphasises the importance of cultures and practices at the heart of sporting 'Gold Mines'.

Management researchers, Jim Collins and Morten Hansen (2011) took a slightly different tack to identify the differentiators between those who are successful, and those who are not. In their book *Great By Choice*, they researched 'matched pairs' (individuals and organizations in the same field, who competed against each other directly and therefore faced the same challenges), such as Antarctic explorers Roald Amundsen and Robert Falcon Scott. Their studies identify the common elements that separate the successful operator from the unsuccessful. Interestingly, their findings also show that innate talent does not tend to be the differentiator. This is a conclusion that sport psychology researcher David Horrocks also shares. His research suggests that the success of world-class sports players, such as Manchester United soccer stars Gary Neville and Denis Irwin, results from their disciplined approach to preparation and practice.

These accounts clearly propose that practice and preparation, rather than innate talent, underpin expertise and high-performance. Whilst that may be true, it does not mean that practice is the only differentiator. As a sport psychologist, I would also ask how people practise and why they practise. What is it that motivates them? Having worked with many elite athletes over years, I also know that they all trained, prepared and practised hard, but only some of them became champions.

An Alternative View

To gain a little more insight, I asked these incredible people what they felt set world-class people apart. What are the key ingredients? What do they notice in other world-class operators? What elements do they think differentiate the very best from the rest?

Adventure racer Bruce Duncan emphasized that the very best performers understand that they will need to make tough choices and be single-minded in pursuit of their goal. In order to do this, Bruce recognizes the importance of being yourself and being confident in yourself. Inevitably this approach tends to separate high achievers from the crowds. Bruce knows that you have to be confident in yourself and your direction, because you'll not make friends with everyone.

England Squash's National Head Coach Chris Robertson knows that world-class squash players are not just technically sound, tactically astute and physically capable. In order to be successful, they must become much more than that. The world's best are normally very measured people, reflective and evaluative in their approach. As such, they are able to take criticism and use it to become better; they have that 'relentless inquisitiveness'. High achievers therefore are constantly looking to develop, to push themselves and learn new things.

> *"Dissatisfaction . . . with where they are, with the state of things. They all realize that this could be better. Contentedness is a terrible thing. They have a relentless compulsion to understand and improve.*
>
> *There is an acceptance that they will always be a little bit frustrated and disappointed but that hasn't for a second dulled their hunger to improve and to learn."*
>
> **James Hoffmann, World Barista Champion,**
> **describing the traits of those who impress him**

Olympic finalist Chris Cook highlights that many of the world's best swimmers are incredibly focused. They have the ability to become completely immersed in the 'here and now'. They understand what they need to do right now. As discussed in earlier chapters, it's likely that the ability to throw yourself into the moment is underpinned by a genuine love for the activity.

> *"You have to relax and enjoy playing well. You need to be sure that this really is what you want to do. You don't want to put in a half- hearted effort for a couple of years. It can be tough. You have to train hard. You have to motivate yourself every day, especially when you're training by yourself."*
>
> **Alison Waters, England International squash player**

No doubt, these proven winners have an intrinsic love for what they do. However, it goes further than that. They also have a love for the challenge. They relish the opportunity to answer questions that they've never answered before, engage in the creative process and to explore the unknown.

> *"I think you have to enjoy the creative process!"*
> **Ben Saunders, record-breaking polar explorer,
> reflecting on overcoming the logistical challenges
> of planning his Antarctic expedition**

As you will no doubt have noticed, there are some common themes within all of these accounts. There are five elements that have been consistently reinforced. As I look through the five, I see a pretty solid recipe for success:

1. Be yourself and be confident in your direction.
2. Be focused on what you need to do right now.
3. Enjoy the process.
4. Be reflective, evaluative and open to criticism.
5. Have that relentless inquisitiveness and compulsion to improve.

The 'Why'

So, what is it that gives world-class people their drive, their focus, their relentless inquisitiveness and their appetite to push the boundaries? I believe that intrinsic enjoyment, love and passion are the catalyst. In the last chapter, we discussed the importance of being true to yourself and following your passion. From personal experience, I know that it is easier said than done. I have learned to recognize my passion by taking a few 'wrong turns' in my journey. I suspect that I am not the only one who has recognized their passion by learning what it is not. In the opening chapter we discussed the role of *luck*.

Perhaps these extremely successful people were lucky enough to recognize their passion fairly early on in their lives. Alan Hinkes knew from the beginning that he loved being outdoors. Alison Waters played squash from the age of five and kept playing because she enjoyed it. Chris Cook dreamed of being an Olympic gold medallist in his childhood. Kenny Atkinson and James Hoffmann both found their love of cooking and coffee, early in their adult lives. James did a number of 'random things' before finding coffee. He knew that selling gas and electricity door to door was not his passion, and so he moved on. When he found coffee, he also found that he didn't need to move on again. Kenny's experience is similar. After he discovered that he was not going to become a pilot, he needed another vocation. He found that cooking was something he could fall in love with. Their experiences show that the intrinsic love and passion can grow. It may start as an interest, but soon become much more than that.

Although many found their passion early in life, it's not the case for everyone. Andy McMenemy was in his mid-40s. He ran his second ever marathon at the age of 45, and went on to complete 'Challenge 66' on his 50th birthday! Andy certainly shows us that it's never too late.

When I reflect on this personally, I could also say that I found my passion fairly early in my adult life. As a student of sport science, I knew that I loved sport psychology and loved working in elite sport with athletes. However, for a few years I became distracted because I was focused on building a business and making my millions.

I suspect that in their heart of hearts, many people know their passion but do not recognize it. Perhaps they don't feel that their passion is valid. I can imagine many housewives asking whether it's legitimate to class motherhood as their passion. What if your passion is not something you can make a living from? What if, like me, you are not sure whether following your passion will fulfil your financial aspirations? What if your passion is a leisure activity? Does it still count? Is it really a good idea to dedicate so much of ourselves to something that might not pay the bills?

For adventure racer Bruce Duncan the answer was simple. He changed his university course to fit in with his passion. He has since structured his career so that he can dedicate his time to adventure racing. In the early years, mountaineer Alan Hinkes earned his living through teaching but spent much of his life climbing. He too made a decision to follow his passion rather than a career in teaching. He has chosen life in the mountains with the risks, the discomfort and the lifestyle that goes with it, ahead of a 'safe' career teaching. Chris Cook chose to follow his passion and his Olympic dream, which often meant that he sacrificed his standard of living. He was aware that, financially, life as a swimmer was not going to be particularly easy. Chris Cook and Ben Saunders have even turned down lucrative sponsorship deals because they were not fully aligned to their passion. In reality, following your passion may require a leap of faith. It may require courage. It could mean that you leave the safe and familiar territory that you're in and step out.

Do you know what your passion is? Do you recognize it? Are you following it? Are you dedicating yourself to it and throwing yourself into it completely? If not, what's stopping you? Is there a fear that you may not 'succeed'? Are you concerned that you might not live up to your own expectations, or the expectations of others? Are you focusing on what you imagine others might think if you did throw yourself into that which you're passionate about? It seems that throwing yourself in fully is a foundation stone of peak performance. Passion gives focus. Our focus often follows our interest. Therefore, the intrinsic love for what we do and the enjoyment we experience are fundamental. Without that, we cannot expect to remain engaged deeply enough to really shine.

> *"Tenacity and perseverance are absolutely vital. You have to be able to deal with the set-backs. Things simply don't go according to plan. There are huge disappointments. To get through that requires you to have the skin of a rhino. You have to believe!"*
> **Linda Conlon, Centre for Life Chief Executive**

Linda makes a very interesting observation. For many people, the prospect of ploughing through reams of scientific data for thousands of hours would appear to be incredibly boring. For most of us, the thought of swimming hour upon hour, up and down a swimming pool, would have the same effect. However, if those things were your passion, they would not seem boring. The fact is, reaching the pinnacle requires an incredible amount of focused effort. To the onlooker, it is tedious. It is 'the drudge'. If there was a factory that produced world-class people, it would look very dull and unappealing from the outside.

Real winners have that passion for what they do, which turns tedious drudge into relentless inquisitiveness. The reason that scientists wade through huge amounts of data is because they are driven to find the answers. The reason that athletes spend countless hours training and practising is because they are searching for the next one hundredth of a second, or the next few centimetres that will give them the edge.

The word passion often conjures up images of men charging into battle, like those scenes in movies such as *Braveheart*.

However, genuine passion and love for what we do often creates a state which seems to be the energetic opposite of charging into battle.

"You have to back off at times and temper your own enthusiasm, and certainly temper your own drive. There is no point in getting killed."
Alan Hinkes, world-leading mountaineer

Equally, ultra-distance runner Andy McMenemy knew that slowing his pace, not speeding up, was crucial to success. In Chapter Four, Andy explained that he had to focus on running below his natural pace, in order to complete all 66 back-to-back ultra-marathons. Patience prevailed over impatience. On many occasions, I have heard leaders in their field describe how their success came because they simply kept going. Their success seems to have come from perseverance, not speed, not inspiration or a sudden flash of brilliance.

Enthusiasm vs Passion

Enthusiasm and passion are not the same thing. Enthusiasm is great but can be short-lived. Personal experience tells me that enthusiasm can give you a great deal of energy but can wane if it is not fuelled by something more substantial. I have often had enthusiasm for new ideas and projects, but if the results that I am looking for don't come pretty quickly, the enthusiasm and energy dissipate.

Enthusiasm can motivate us, as can many things. Need often motivates us, as we have discussed. Desires motivate us. However, many of those have a shelf life. If we are motivated by need, that motivation will dry up when there is no longer a need. We've seen how some world-class athletes lose the hunger when they achieve their financial goals. The same is true of desire. In fact, if we stop believing that our needs or desires will be met through a task, we lose our motivation to do it. Understanding what motivates and drives us is incredibly valuable if we wish to perform to our maximum.

What are you motivated by? Why do you currently do the things you do? Is it because you're driven by need? Are you chasing your current desires? Or is your motivation for what you do driven by passion? A great way to test is to eliminate possibilities. If you won hundreds of millions in the Lotto, would you still do what you do? If we took away the need or desire for greater financial wealth, would we also take away the motivation? If we gave Alan Hinkes a hundred million pounds, I don't think he'd stop climbing mountains. Equally, if we gave Bruce Duncan a huge sum of money, I don't think he'd stop adventure racing. Chris Cook decided not to take a six-figure sponsorship deal because it would not help him swim two lengths of the swimming pool quicker.

Another interesting test of motivation is to see whether you're able to focus on the next step. In my life to date, I have often found it tough to focus on one step at a time. When this happens, I find it is because I have begun to focus on the outcome. That's a really powerful sign that my motivation is strongly tied to the outcome, rather than to the process. Unlike the outcome, the process happens one moment at a time. The process happens in this moment, the here and now. If I am genuinely interested in the process, that's where my focus will be drawn. Focus follows interest. If I am interested in the outcome, my focus will be drawn to it. At this very moment, as I type these words, I am in an unusual position. My need and my passion are slightly in conflict. My need states that I should focus my energies on generating consultancy business for the coming months. I should be trying to fill the gaps I have in my diary. However, my passion pulls me into writing. In this moment, I am interested in transferring the thoughts and feelings that I wish to communicate into writing. I'm not sure what the outcome of this will be, but I am fully engaged in the process.

The Next One Per Cent

Reflecting on our motivation is a very worthwhile starting point in our own personal quest to excel. However, it is just the start. We can also reflect on many of the other questions that have been raised by the incredibly successful people I have interviewed. For example, when do you compromise? Which of the tiny little details do you not pick up on? When do you say, 'Ah, that will do, it'll be okay'? Through my work I have learned to listen to the language people use because it helps me detect world-class operators. I have not heard those at the pinnacle of their field say the words, 'it'll do' because they never seem to feel that way. As James Hoffmann mentioned, these people often have that 'dis-satisfied' quality that makes them hunt for the ways that they can improve. The people that excel, seem to know what it takes to get an extra one or two per cent in their performance right now. They know the little things that can be done because they are always looking for them. They are always asking questions and seeking more understanding about how to improve.

Sport psychology researcher David Horrocks (in press) noticed similar traits in *über elite* athletes. One of the players he studied was Manchester United and England footballer Gary Neville. Through his research, David Horrocks found that Gary Neville's training, practice and preparation pattern was different from many other professional players. Neville would spend many hours each day, outside of training, watching video footage of the opponent and mentally preparing for the next game. He would study the opposing team, not just the man he would face directly. This would enable Neville to understand how the ball tends to get to his opposite number, who passes to him, what type of passes are used, which passes opposing players can make comfortably and which they tend not to.

Interestingly, many people remark that truly elite sports players are often 'in the right place at the right time'. If, through studying footage, you understand where the ball tends to land, it is more likely that you'll be 'in the right place at the right time'. Many of those things that are often attributed to 'luck' may in fact be the result of planning and preparation.

Are You Scott or Amundsen?

If we compare the successful Antarctic explorer Roald Amundsen with his arguably more famous, but less successful, counterpart Robert Falcon Scott we see a similar pattern. Amundsen was not only the first to reach the South Pole, but also survived the return journey. Scott, by comparison, reached the pole over a month after Amundsen and perished (along with his team) on the way home. Roland Huntford (1999) analyzed the differences in the approaches taken by the two men in his book, *The Last Place On Earth*. His study suggests that the difference in their result was not down to 'luck'. Amundsen's preparation and planning was extensive. He served an apprenticeship with the Eskimo and practiced their methods. He was able to draw on the Eskimo's vast experience of living in polar environments. As a result, he gained a valuable insight into the tiny details that make all the difference. Amundsen learned the importance of reducing perspiration, because moisture freezes in sub-zero temperatures. Therefore, he opted for loose fitting clothing (to increase evaporation) and chose to move relatively slowly. He also chose to use dogs and sleds, which have been tried and tested in polar environments for centuries. In addition, Amundsen reasoned that some of the dogs would inevitably perish, but that they could be used as food for the other dogs in the pack.

By comparison, Scott opted to use ponies and motorized sleds. Neither had been extensively tested or used in a polar environment. The ponies perished and the engines of the sleds froze and cracked. Scott and his team ended up pulling the sleds themselves, which no doubt caused them to sweat profusely. In addition, Scott took one tonne of supplies for a team of 17 men. Amundsen took three tonnes for five men. Amundsen also marked each of his supply depots with many flags, which gave him a 10-kilometre target, should he lose his bearings slightly. His flags were black, to make them visible against a white background. Scott placed a single flag at each supply depot making it far harder to identify. Ironically, Scott's remains were found within just a few miles of a supply depot.

There are dozens of examples such as these. They tell us that Amundsen prepared for the most extreme of eventualities, accounted for the error-margins and built in considerable insurance policies. Captain Scott, on the other hand, cursed his 'misfortune'.

Your Next One Per Cent

What could you do to improve right now? How can you gain one or two per cent? As I reviewed the first draft of this book, I became aware of sentences that needed to be tightened up, and saw extra references that could be added. I also found that I needed to trim some sections and add a little more explanation to others. When I wrote my first book, *Peak Performance*

Every Time, I found that I constantly read and re-read sections, making changes because they were never quite right.

As I submitted the final manuscript, I would have said that the book was as good as I could have made it at that moment . . . but it was not perfect. Towards the end I did start to recognize that some of the changes required a pretty big effort for a relatively small return. On occasions I was tempted not to make the changes but to say, 'Ah, that'll do, it's pretty good now'. For many people, I believe that is where they differentiate themselves from world-class people. Those who have reached a truly elite standard accept that as you climb the ladder, a one per cent gain requires an awful lot more effort than it did at the beginning. There is a point in time when the effort starts to outweigh the return. At that point, lots of people stop making the changes. They stop doing the tiny things that world-class people do. The title of this chapter is *Be The Best You Can Be*. The first question is 'how can you become truly exceptional?' The very simple answer that I proposed is, 'do what exceptional people do'. They pick up as many of the tiny details as they possibly can, regardless of the effort it takes to get them right, because they know that those tiny details do matter. Sometimes, getting that extra one or two per cent requires us to really push ourselves. Pushing ourselves can be uncomfortable, sometimes even painful. Many people stop pushing at the point where things become uncomfortable. When I am exercising, I will take a step or two into discomfort but won't tend to go much further than that. I don't have any reason to go beyond mild discomfort. I enjoy stretching myself and I enjoy a challenge, but I am not a fan of physical pain. When I was in training for a specific event, I was much more willing to experience discomfort. I would naturally push further into my discomfort zone because there was a reason to. On one occasion I ran a half marathon for charity. I knew that I wasn't going to run a half marathon with no training. I also knew that if I only ever did two or three miles, I would not allow my body to adapt to running 13 miles, so I had to push myself. Although I was not focused on achieving a specific time, I wanted to run well so I challenged myself in training. I had a reason to journey further into the discomfort zone, but often stopped when I felt pain. Although the event held importance to me, it was not important enough to warrant the pain in my opinion. Exceptional people often do venture into painful territory. They do take enormous risks and they do it because their passion is a strong enough force to carry them through.

Is Failing Really Failure?

As we have seen through the course of this book, world-class people are willing to try and fail. I often see this as a differentiator between those at the pinnacle of their field and the rest. Most of us are happy to try something a few times. But, how many people will continually attempt things and continually fail? How many failures would you be willing to experience before you quit? How long would it take for you to say, 'I can't do this, it's pointless, I'm stopping'? How long before you'd conclude that it was too difficult or impossible? Could you try and fail 20 times? How about 50 or 100? How about 1000? Would you be willing to try and fail if your failure was public? Could you stand up in front of millions of viewers and give it your all, knowing that you could fail in your attempt? Where would you draw the line? What would stop you? Would you be concerned about what other people thought? Would your own self-judgement be the barrier? Are you tying yourself to an outcome, and therefore a need for success? If so, why is the outcome important to you? Do you need the outcome to boost your self-worth? Would you still have the motivation if we took the outcome away?

The answers to these questions show us the difference in mentality between those who have reached the pinnacle and those who have not. As we have seen, high achievers do embrace failure and mistakes. They don't seem to have the same hang ups as the rest of us because they seem not to be tied as closely to the outcome. Failure has a different meaning to the exceptional people I interviewed. To some people, failure is the catalyst for negative self-judgement. To others, it is an opportunity to improve. Many people who experience failure will try to avoid the negative judgements by employing excuses. They prefer to blame external factors rather than taking responsibility themselves. How do you respond to failures? When do you take responsibility and when are you reluctant to? Do you take full responsibility, both publically and privately?

I am often dismayed to see football (soccer) managers in the UK who consistently seem to blame everyone and everything else for their team's performance. There are very few who publically say, 'I got it wrong' or 'we got it wrong'. Those managers who are willing to take responsibility are a breath of fresh air in my opinion. Some will say that they were beaten by a better team, but few will publically recognize that there were things that they need to do better. Unfortunately, when the manager fails to take responsibility, it sends a message to their team; blame other people. It tells the team that blame is fine, excuses are okay and that our performance is not under our control. Rather than looking at themselves and making changes when things go wrong, these people tend to pray for a change of luck. That doesn't strike me as a particularly great strategy! Interestingly, during the first Be World-Class Conference Keir Worth told delegates that to remain world-class required 'a brutal honesty' and the ability to hold your hand up and say 'I got that wrong'.

What is Success?

Excuses appear when we don't take responsibility. Sometimes we might use the excuses as a way of protecting our ego or self-worth. We don't want it to be our fault because it could have an impact on the way we feel about our self. As we discussed in Chapter Eight, people often rely on outcomes and results to fuel their self-worth. Arguably, this happens when there is a hole in our self-worth, which we are trying to fill. Some people try to convince themself that they're okay if they have a big house, a decent car, a gold medal or a healthy bank account. If those things are lacking, the hole becomes visible. Perhaps this is a symptom of what Viktor Frankl (2004) refers to as an 'existential vacuum'.

However, filling that hole with 'successes', arguably provides a false cure. It's like taking a painkiller for a headache. In the words of a friend of mine, 'a headache is not an aspirin deficiency'. The way to cure a headache is sometimes to rehydrate, or maybe to rest, or to drink less caffeine or get some fresh air. Perhaps, the way to fill the hole in our self-worth is to recognize it for what it really is and then address the issue. Perhaps we need to recognize that we are good enough without the outcome. Maybe we need to understand that we are good enough anyway. Those things that are fundamentally part of who we are will not change according to the car we drive, the house we live in, the money in our wallets or the medals around our necks. We don't become a better person when we earn more money, jump further, swim faster or score more goals. Equally, we are no worse if those things reduce. It's easier said than done, I know. I grapple with these challenges too!

Getting to know yourself is arguably a life-long journey, which I suspect has no definitive end. As we become more critically self-reflective, we might start to identify those times that we do create a façade. Which bits are we trying to hide or disguise? Which bits are we not too proud of, and why is it that we're not proud of them? Do you try to create a mask that shows the world how financially successful you are, even when you're struggling? Do you do that because you're not proud of the fact you're struggling? Have you subscribed to the theory that having more money equals success. Do you also believe that success is 'good' and failure is 'bad'? Do you try to cover up your failures or make excuses for them?

I believe that this cultural perception (i.e. that success is 'good' and that failure is 'bad') prevents many people from achieving their potential. The fear of failure becomes a real barrier because 'failing' impacts on self-worth. I have seen people dedicate far more energy into 'appearing successful' than they do into becoming successful. In the desperate fight to keep up with the Joneses, they actually step away from being themselves, following their passion and becoming the best that they can be. Perhaps we choose social and cultural conformity over personal fulfilment?

Self-Knowledge

As we delve deeper, we might also start to become aware of our deeper self, of those things that can become our Achilles heel. I believe that there is a magic trio, which I often call the three amigos. When this trio is present, we tend to perform really well. That trio is made up of confidence, motivation and focus. These work together and are inter-dependent. They feed off each other and can build positive spirals of performance. However, there is another trio that can cause problems for us. Existential psychologists, such as Irvin Yalom (1999), also rec-ognize a trio that is comprised of anger, fear and guilt. In my experience, these three also feed off each other and can set off a downward spiral. I have often found that anger follows fear, and that fear is tied to guilt. This relationship is recognized by other eminent psychologists such as Stephen Diamond, Rollo May and Viktor Frankl. When things don't go our way, sometimes we feel angry. That anger is often underpinned by fear and guilt. In order to disarm these three, we often need to resolve them through forgiveness! I can see us needing courage for this one too.

If you genuinely wish to embark on your own journey to reach your full potential, you need to recognize that it is a journey, not simply a destination. The journey is necessary. It is integral. We cannot go around it, over it, under it or catch a bus to avoid taking it. Knowing this, it's probably wise to embark on it with a smile. It is not a race or a competition. There are no prizes for first place or judges holding up score cards. Enjoy the journey. Take in the sights. Engage with every step and embrace the thrills and challenges along the way. The journey to become truly exceptional is really just a part of the journey through life. If we're honest, there is only one destination in the journey of life and it's called *the end*. Perhaps the whole point in this thing we call 'life' is to enjoy the journey and experience all it has to offer, to engage with it and to literally *live* it. Arguably, that is the same with the journey to becoming the best *you* can be.

So what can we learn about that journey from these world-class people?

If I could sum up what I've learned in one sentence it would be this . . .

Do what you love and love what you do.

Bibliography

Ankersen, R. (2011) *The Gold Mine Effect: Unlocking The Essence of World Class Performance*, London: Rasmus Ankersen.

Aristotle (trans. 1984) *Complete Works of Aristotle, Volume 1: The Revised Oxford Translation*, Princeton, NJ: Princeton University Press.

Bandura, A. (1997) *Self-efficacy: The Exercise of Control*, New York: Worth Publishers.

Baumeister, R.F. and Showers, C.J. (1986) A review of paradoxical performance effects: Choking under pressure in sports and mental tests, *European Journal of Social Psychology*, 16(4), 361–383.

Be World Class Conference (2011) Bruce Duncan . . . on Mental Toughness, 6th October 2011. Online. Available http://www.beworldclass.tv (accessed 31st January 2012).

Be World Class Conference (2011) Chris Cook . . . on Talent, 6th October 2011. Online. Available http://www.beworldclass.tv (accessed 31st January 2012).

Be World Class Conference (2011) James Hoffmann . . . on the Finest Details, 6th October 2011. Online. Available http://www.beworldclass.tv (accessed 31st January 2012).

Be World Class Conference (2011) Keir Worth . . . on Staying Ahead, 6th October 2011. Online. Available http://www.beworldclass.tv (accessed 31st January 2012).

Be World Class Conference (2011) Kenny Atkinson . . . on Standards, 6th October 2011. Online. Available http://www.beworldclass.tv (accessed 31st January 2012).

Beilock, S. (2010) *Choke*, New York: Free Press.

Black, K. and Damon, J. (2010) *Attention to Detail: A Look at Walt Disney World Parks*, Charleston, SC: CreateSpace.

Bleill, J. and Tabb, M. (2010) *One Step at a Time: A Young Marine's Story of Courage, Hope and a New Life in the NFL*, Chicago, IL: Triumph Books.

Bond, F.W. and Flaxman, P.E. (2006) The ability of psychological flexibility and job control to predict learning, job performance, and mental health, *Journal of Organizational Behavior Management*, 26, 113–130.

Bonneville-Roussy, A. and Vallerand, R.J. (2007) Passion and performance: A look at expert performers. Paper presented at the 3rd International Congress on Self-Determination Theory (SDT), Toronto, Ontario, Canada.

Bray, S.R. and Brawley, L.R. (2002a) Role Efficacy, Role Clarity and Role Performance Effectiveness, *Small Group Research*, 33(2), 233–253.

Bray, S.R. and Brawley, L.R. (2002b) Efficacy for Independent Role Functions: Evidence from the Sport Domain, *Small Group Research*, 33(6), 644–666.

Carragher, J. (2011) Fear of failure undermines England, BBC Sport, 28th June 2011. Online. Available http://news.bbc.co.uk/sport1/hi/football/13929349.stm (accessed 28th June 2011).

Clash, J.M. (2003) *Forbes to the Limits: Pushing Yourself to the Edge in Adventure and in Business*, New York: John Wiley & Sons Inc.

Collins, J. and Hansen, M.T. (2011) *Great by Choice*, London: Random House.

Colvin, G. (2008) *Talent is Overrated: What Really Separates World Class Performers from Everybody Else*, New York: Portfolio.

Corlett, J. (1996) Virtue Lost: Courage in Sport, *Journal of Philosophy of Sport*, 23(1), 45–55.

Covey, S.R. (2004) *The 7 Habits of Highly Effective People*, New York: Simon & Schuster.

Coyle, D. (2009) *The Talent Code: Unlocking the Secret of Skill in Maths, Art, Music, Sport, and Just About Everything Else*, New York: Random House.

Csikszentmihalyi, M. (1990) *Flow: The Psychology of Optimal Experience*, New York: Harper and Row.

Deci, E.L. and Ryan, R.M. (2000) The 'what' and 'why' of goal pursuits: Human needs and the self-determination of behavior, *Psychological Inquiry*, 11, 227–268.

Deci, E.L. and Ryan, R.M. (2002) *Handbook of Self-Determination Research*, Rochester: University of Rochester Press.

Diamond, S.A. (2009) What is existential therapy? in Leeming, D.A., Madden, K. and Marlan, S. (eds) *Encyclopedia of Psychology and Religion* (pp. 304–305) New York, NY: Springer Verlag.

Dilman, I. (1999) *Free Will*, London: Routledge.

Donnelly, J.H. and Ivancevich, J.M. (1975) Role Clarity and the Salesman, *Journal of Marketing*, 39(1), 71–74.

Ericsson, K.A. and Charness, N. (1999) Expert Performance: Its Structure and Acquisition, in Ceci, S.J. and Williams, W.M. (eds) *The Nature-Nurture Debate: The Essential Readings*, New York: Wiley.

Flegal, K. and Anderson, M. (2008) Overthinking skilled motor performance, *Psychonomic Bulletin & Review*, 15, 927–932.

Frankl, V.E. (2004) *Man's Search for Meaning*, London: Rider.

Gallwey, T. (1986) *The Inner Game of Tennis*, London: Pan Books.

Gallwey, T. (2003) *The Inner Game of Work*, New York: Texere Publishing.

Gladwell, M. (2008) *Outliers: The Story of Success*, London: Little, Brown & Co.

Halden-Brown, S. (2003) *Mistakes Worth Making: How to Turn Sports Errors into Athletic Excellence*, Champaign, IL: Human Kinetics.

Harford, T. (2011) *Adapt: Why Success Always Starts with Failure*, London: Little Brown.

Hartley, S.R. (2011a) *Peak Performance Every Time*, London: Routledge.

Hartley, S.R. (2011b) Two Lengths of the Pool: A case study of what a leading UK law firm learned from elite sport, *Choice*, 9(2), 45–46.

Heath, R. (2009) *Celebrating Failure: The Power of Taking Risks, Making Mistakes and Thinking Big*, New Jersey: Career Press.

Horrocks, D. (in press) Cognitive Aspects of Deliberate Practice, *Journal of Sport Psychology in Action* – Manuscript ID USPA-2011-0049.

Horrocks, D. and Lawrence, I. (in press) Professional Soccer and Elite Level Preparation: A case study of a 'healthy perfectionist', *Qualitative Research in Sport and Exercise* – Manuscript ID RQRS-2011-0121.

Huntford, R. (1999) *The Last Place on Earth*, New York: Modern Library.

Jackson, S. and Csikszentmihalyi, M. (1999) *Flow in Sports*, Champaign, IL: Human Kinetics.

Jauncey, P. (2002) *Managing Yourself and Others*, Brisbane: Copy-Right Publishing.

Johnson, M. (1996) *Slaying the Dragon: How to Turn Your Small Steps into Great Feats*, New York: HarperCollins.

Kase, L. (2008) *The Confident Leader*, New York: McGraw-Hill.

Kloosterman, P. (1988) Self Confidence and Motivation in Mathematics, *Journal of Educational Psychology*, 80(3), 345–351.

Knight, C.F. and Dyer, D. (2005) *Performance without Compromise: How Emerson Consistently Achieves Winning Results*, Boston, MA: Harvard Business Press.

Lindsley, D.H., Brass, D.J. and Thomas, J.B. (1995) Efficacy-Performance Spirals: A Multilevel Perspective, *Academy of Management Review*, 20(3), 645–678.

Lowenstein, G. (1994) The Psychology of Curiosity: A Review and Reinterpretation, *Psychological Bulletin*, 116(1), 75–88.

Maddi, S.R. (2006) Hardiness: The courage to grow from stress, *Journal of Positive Psychology*, 1, 160–168.

Maher, C.A. (2005) *School Sport Psychology*, Oxford, UK: Haworth Press.

Manz, C.C. (2000) *Emotional Discipline: The Power to Choose How You Feel*, San Francisco: Berrett-Koehler.

Manz, C.C. (2002) *The Power of Failure*, San Francisco: Berrett-Koehler.

Martin Fischer, J. and Ravizza, M. (1998) *Responsibility and Control: A Theory of Moral Responsibility*, Cambridge: Cambridge University Press.

May, R. (1953) *Man's Search for Himself*, New York: W.W. Norton & Co.

May, R. (1975) *The Courage to Create*, New York: W.W. Norton & Co.

McDonald, J., Orlick, T. and Letts, M. (1995) Mental readiness in surgeons and its links to performance excellence in surgery, *Journal of Pediatric Orthopedics*, 15(5), 691–697.

Michelli, J.A. (2008) *The New Gold Standard: 5 Leadership Principles for Creating a Legendary Customer Experience Courtesy of the Ritz-Carlton Hotel Company*, New York: McGraw-Hill.

Millar, D. (2011) *Racing Through the Dark: The Fall and Rise of David Millar*, London: Orion.

Moore, R. (2011) *Sky's the Limit: British Cycling's Quest to Conquer the Tour de France*, London: HarperCollins.

Murphy, L. (2011) Why service not size should be focus from ambitious firms, *Yorkshire Post*, 11th October 2011. Online. Available http://www.yorkshirepost.co.uk/business/business-news/why_service_not_size_should_be_focus_for_ambitious_firms_1_3858539. (accessed 27th October 2011).

Neff, K.D. (2009) The Role of Self-Compassion in Development: A Healthier Way to Relate to Oneself, *Human Development*, 52, 211–214.

Newman, B.M. and Newman, P.R. (2008) *Development Through Life: A Psychosocial Approach*, Belmont, CA: Wadsworth.

Pelham, B.W. (1991) On confidence and consequence: The certainty and importance of self-knowledge, *Journal of Personality and Social Psychology*, 60(4), 518–530.

Ravizza, K. and Hanson, T. (1998) *Heads-up Baseball: Playing the Game One Pitch at a Time*, Columbus, OH: McGraw Hill.

Reitman, E.E. and Williams, C.D. (1961) Relationships between hope of success and fear of failure, anxiety, and need for achievement, *The Journal of Abnormal and Social Psychology*, 62(2), 465–467.

Reker, G.T., Peacock, E.J. and Wong, P.T.P. (1987) Meaning and purpose in life and well being: A life-span perspective, *Journal of Gerontology*, 42, 44–49.

Richtel, M. (2010) Multi-tasking hurts brain's ability to focus, scientists say, *Seattle Times*, June 6th 2010.

Ross, D. (2010) *George and Robert Stephenson: A Passion for Success*, Stroud: The History Press.

Seligman, M.E.P. (2005) *Authentic Happiness: Using the New Positive Psychology to Realize your Potential for Lasting Fulfillment*, New York: Free Press.

Sheard, M. (2012) *Mental Toughness: The Mind-set Behind Sporting Achievement* (2nd Edition), London: Routledge.

Smith, S. and Wheeler, J. (2002) *Managing Customer Experience: Turning Customers into Advocates*, Indianapolis, IN: FT Press.

Syed, M. (2011) *Bounce: The Myth of Talent and the Power of Practice*, London: Forth Estate.

Taylor, J. and Wilson, G.S. (2005) *Applying Sport Psychology: Four Perspectives*, Champaign, IL: Human Kinetics.

TED Talks (2009) Bill Gates Q&A with Chris Anderson. 6th February 2009. Online. Available http://blog.ted.com/2009/02/06/bill_gates_qa_w/ (accessed 8th June 2011).

Tesser, A., Wood, J.V. and Stapel, D.A. (2005) *On Building, Defending and Regulating the Self: A Psychological Perspective*, New York: Psychology Press.

Tolle, E. (1999) *Practicing the Power of Now*, Novato, CA: New World Library.

Torres, D. and Weil, E. (2009) *Age is Just a Number: Achieve Your Dreams at Any Age in Your Life*, New York: Crown Archetypes.

Trimble, V. (1993) *Overnight Success: FedEx and Frederick Smith, Its Renegade Creator*, New York: Crown.

Trout, J. and Rivkin, S. (1998) *The Power of Simplicity*, Columbus, OH: McGraw Hill.

Vallerand, R.J. (2008) On the psychology of passion: In search of what makes people's lives most worth living, *Canadian Psychology*, 49, 1–13.

Vallerand, R.J., Portier, M.S. and Guay, F. (1997) Self-determination and persistence in a real-life setting: Toward a motivational model of high school dropout, *Journal of Personality and Social Psychology*, 72, 1161–1176.

Weissman, D.H., Roberts, K.C., Visscher, K.M. and Woldorff, M.G. (2006) The neural bases of momentary lapses in attention, *Nature Neuroscience*, 9, 971–978.

White, A.A.K. (2009) *From Comfort Zone to Performance Management*, New York: White & MacLean Publishing.

Wiggins-Dohlvik, K., Stewart, R.M., Babbitt, R.J., Gelfond, J., Zarzabal, L.A. and Willis, R.E. (2009) Surgeons' performance during critical situations: competence, confidence, and composure, *American Journal of Surgery*, 198(6), 817–23.

Wong, P.T.P. and Fry, P.S. (1989) (eds) *The Human Quest for Meaning: A Handbook of Psychological Research and Clinical Applications*, London: Routledge.

Yalom, I.D. (1999) *Momma and the Meaning of Life*, New York: Basic Books.

About Simon Hartley

Simon Hartley is an experienced sport psychologist and performance coach. He helps athletes and business people to get their mental game right. During the last 15 years, Simon has worked with gold medalists, world record holders, top 5 world ranked professional athletes and championship winning teams. He has worked at the highest level of sport, including spells in Premiership football, Premiership rugby union, First Class County Cricket, Super League, golf, tennis, motor sport and with Great British Olympians.

Since 2005, Simon has also applied the principles of sport psychology to business, education, healthcare and the charity sector. This has included projects with some of the world's leading corporations and foremost executives.

2011 saw the publication of Simon's first book, *Peak Performance Every Time*, and the delivery of the first ever Be World-Class Conference.

Index

20 Mile Marching 49

Adidas 65
Amundsen, Roald 152, 162–3
anger 168–9
Aristotle 15
Armstrong, Lance 10
Atkinson, Kenny 3–4, 6, 8, 12,
    21–2, 24, 26, 32–3, 48–9,
    55–6, 61, 64, 77, 78, 86–7,
    105, 112, 113, 116, 139,
    145, 156
attention to detail 72–3
authenticity 141–2

basics, perfecting 55–7
Beckham, David 28
blame 131–3
boundaries, setting 96–9
brick walls 114–16

Candy, John 144
Centre for Life 83–5
Challenge 66 17, 47, 60, 108,
    156
Champs, The 112
commitment 116–17
compromise, no 63–81
confidence 131–2

Confucius 51
Conlon, Linda 5, 20–1, 36,
    83–5, 96, 158
control 116, 123–33s
Cook, Chris 4, 6–7, 8, 13,
    16–17, 23, 39–40, 48, 57–9,
    60, 64–5, 74, 87, 88–9,
    92–3, 94, 95–6, 110–11,
    117, 126, 127, 136, 139,
    154, 156, 157, 160
Cooke, Nicole 136
Cool Runnings (movie) 144
courage 99–101, 148
creativity 99, 144–5
curiosity 79–80

deliberate practice 25–6
detail
    attention to 72–3
    awareness of 78–9
    confidence and 73–4
    critical, understanding
        75–8
dreams 15–24
Duncan, Bruce 4, 9, 10, 22, 23,
    25, 35, 52, 63, 70, 90, 94,
    105, 107, 114, 116, 125,
    139–40, 148–9, 153, 157,
    160

effectiveness, simplicity and
60–2
ego 127–9, 131
enthusiasm vs passion 159–61
existentialism 116

failure 101–2, 165–6
as catalyst for success 88–9
fear of 141–2
preparedness for 86–7
fear 168–9
FedEx 56–7
Flow State 42
focus 43–5
mistakes and 89–91
Frankl, Viktor 19, 117–18, 123,
130, 138, 167

Gates, Bill 9, 10
Gillingham, Nick 16
goal-setting 40–2
guilt 168–9

Hardiness Construct 116
Haworth, Nigel 139
Hinkes, Alan 5, 9, 10, 17, 21,
23, 26–7, 28, 33, 37–8, 43,
51, 66–8, 72–3, 80, 106,
109, 112, 116, 124, 127,
141, 148, 149, 156, 159,
160
Hoffmann, James 4, 7, 8, 17, 65,
75, 76–7, 78, 79, 90–1,
97–9, 110, 154, 156, 161

Irwin, Denis 153

Karnazes, Dean 17
KISS principle (Keep It
Stupidly Simple) 51

learning, responsibility and
126–7
limits 118–21, 146–8
Logotherapy 118
love
power of 32–4
of the process 45–6
luck 132,155–6
talent and 151–3

Matthew, Nick 11–12, 104
McMenemy, Andy 5, 8, 17–19,
33, 47–8, 60–1, 65–6, 71,
108, 114, 116, 125, 126,
142, 149, 156, 159
mental toughness 103–21
mistakes
effect on confidence 91–3
effect on focus and
motivation 89–91
moment, being in 42–5
Moorehouse, Adrian 16
motivation 30–1, 159–61
mistakes and 89–91

need vs passion 27–8
Neville, Gary 153, 161–2
Norris, Lieutenant Tommy
119–20

opportunity, talent and 10–14
optimal intrinsic motivation 42

passion 20–1, 25–7, 148–9
  aligning dreams and
    31–2
  vs enthusiasm 159–61
  foundation of 135–6
  vs need 27–8
  power of 25–7, 136–7
  recognition of 154–9
PDA cycle 43
Pierre-White, Marco 24
psychological flexibility 37
purpose. strength of 66–8

reason 22–5, 28–31, 155–9
Redmoon, Ambrose 148
resilience 105
responsibility 123–33
  learning and 126–7
Rhodes, Gary 24
Ridgway, John 10, 22–3
Robertson, Chris 4, 11, 33,
    43–4, 104, 112, 113,
    129–30, 153–4
Robertson, Simon
    17–18
role clarity 54
Rolf, Susan 127–8
Ronaldinho 144
Ronaldo 144
Rossi, Gary 5, 7–8, 44–5, 56,
    57, 73, 105, 115, 116, 119,
    148
Roux brothers 24

sacrifice 23
Safin, Marat 27, 144

Saunders, Ben 5, 9–10, 22–3,
    35, 47, 51–2, 64, 85–6, 90,
    91, 95, 101–2, 110, 125,
    132–3, 138, 155, 157
Scott, Robert Falcon 152, 162,
    163
self-awareness 137
self-belief 117, 138–41,
    148
self-criticality 129
self-discipline 146
self-knowledge 137, 146,
    149,168–9
self-reflection 146
self-responsibility 129–30,
    146
self-sufficiency 146
self-worth 143–4
simplicity 51–62
SMaC recipe (Specific,
    Measurable and
    Consistent) 55
SMARTER goals 41
Smith, Fred 56–7
strategy, tactics and execution
    36–8
success
  definition 167–8
  dreams and 15
  failure as catalyst for 88–9

tactics 36–8
talent
  and luck 151–3
  and opportunity 10–14
task clarity 54

Thornton, Michael E. 119–20, 148

trapdoor 143–4

uncertainty 95–6

walls 114–16

Walt Disney World Resorts 69

Waters, Alison 4, 10–11, 41, 53, 64, 70, 88, 89, 123–4, 140, 141, 154, 156

Worth, Keir 4, 11, 12, 36, 41–2, 53, 55, 61, 68, 69, 100–1, 104, 113, 166

Young, Chris 97

Zone, The 42, 136

Index compiled by Annette Musker